YO, SLOTH.

I GOT THE FACTS.

Eddie Watts

CONTENTS

INTRODUCTION

Picture your fridge.
You see it?
Great.

Hopefully, it's full.

And here's why: a full fridge is more energy-efficient than an empty one. Cold items help maintain low temperatures and reduce the workload on the compressor.

That's a scientific fact, and one that gives you permission (purse allowing) to go load up on groceries.

Did you see what I just did? I quietly gave you something to ponder.

That's what this book is here to do: to enlighten, to entertain, and to deliver "Wait, what?" conversation.

Turns out, sparking curiosity is enough.

You just need to spark curiosity.

On that front, this book's got you covered.

Ready? Let's go.

CHAPTER ONE

ORDINARY OBJECTS, EXTRAORDINARY STORIES

THE MAN WHO ATE AN AIRPLANE

M ost people see an airplane and think of travel. Michel Lotito saw lunch.

Known as "Monsieur Mangetout" (French for "Mr. Eat-All"), Lotito made a career out of eating things that should have landed him in a hospital. His meals included bicycles, shopping carts, TVs, and even a coffin. But his crowning achievement? A full-size Cessna 150 airplane.

Lotito spent two years (1978-1980) consuming the aircraft, piece by piece, washing down up to two pounds of metal per day with mineral oil and water. His Guinness World Record plaque celebrated his "strangest diet." He then ate that too.

How did he survive? Lotito had a rare condition called pica, which causes cravings for non-food items. His stomach lining was twice as thick as normal, and his gastric acid could dissolve metal. Essentially, his digestive system was built like a human garbage disposal.

Despite his diet of glass, nails, and bolts, Lotito never suffered serious internal injuries. Bananas and eggs, though? Those upset his stomach.

THE GREAT RUBBER DUCK ESCAPE

In 1992, a shipping container carrying 28,000 rubber ducks was lost at sea, setting off one of the most fascinating accidental experiments in oceanography. Known as the "Friendly Floatees," these ducks drifted across the world's oceans, helping scientists track currents and better understand oceanic circulation.

The spill occurred when a cargo ship traveling from Hong Kong to the U.S. hit rough waters, sending a container full of bath toys into the Pacific Ocean. The ducks proved remarkably resilient, traveling thousands of miles over the years. Some washed up on Alaskan shores within months, while others circumnavigated the Arctic and reached the U.K. and even Australia.

Oceanographer Curtis Ebbesmeyer studied ocean currents using the ducks' movements. These unexpected research assistants provided valuable insights into how plastic pollution travels and how oceanic gyres, massive rotating current systems, influence global water movement.

Today, giant inflatable rubber ducks float in harbors worldwide, from Sydney to Hong Kong. What started as a shipping accident ended up reshaping how scientists map the ocean.

THE SWEET ACCIDENT THAT LED TO THE MICROWAVE

In 1945, engineer Percy Spencer wasn't trying to revolutionize cooking. He was working on radar technology at Raytheon when his chocolate bar mysteriously melted in his pocket. The culprit? Microwaves emitted by an active magnetron, a device used in radar systems. Instead of tossing his gooey snack, Spencer got curious. If microwaves could melt chocolate, what else could they do?

He tested his theory with popcorn kernels, and soon his lab was filled with fluffy explosions. Next, he placed an egg near the magnetron. It burst in a colleague's face. Spencer and his team at Raytheon developed the first microwave oven, the Radarange.

But this was no countertop gadget. It weighed 750 pounds, cost $3,000, and was used primarily in restaurants and commercial kitchens. It wasn't until the 1970s that microwaves became affordable and compact.

All of it traces back to a melted candy bar and a messy pocket.

PIZZA IN SPACE: A COSMIC CRAVING

In 2001, Pizza Hut became the first company to deliver a pizza beyond Earth, sending a salami-topped pie to the International Space Station. The cost: $1 million, making it the most expensive pizza delivery in history.

Because traditional pizza would fall apart in microgravity, scientists modified the recipe, using extra-thick dough and reducing moisture in the sauce and cheese. Pepperoni was out since it spoiled too quickly, so salami became the official topping of the cosmos. Russian cosmonauts were the lucky taste testers.

NASA has also experimented with 3D-printed pizza as a potential food source for astronauts on deep space missions. These futuristic pizzas are printed layer by layer and cooked in minutes.

Pizza started in Naples. It has now been to space. That's a solid run.

THE ACCIDENTAL INVENTION OF BUBBLE WRAP

Bubble wrap wasn't supposed to protect packages. It was meant to be wallpaper. In 1957, engineers Alfred Fielding and Marc Chavannes tried to create textured wallpaper by sealing two shower curtains together and trapping air inside. The result was a bubbly plastic sheet that nobody wanted on their walls.

They pitched it as greenhouse insulation next. Another flop. The real breakthrough came in 1961, when IBM needed a way to ship its new, fragile computers safely. Bubble wrap wasn't about decorating walls. It was about protecting valuable cargo. IBM became their first big customer, and bubble wrap became a packaging staple. Today the industry is worth over $10 billion.

The best part, though? Popping it. Studies show that popping bubble wrap can lower stress and boost mood. There's even a holiday for it. Bubble Wrap Appreciation Day, every January.

Not bad for a couple of shower curtains.

HOW A MISTAKE GAVE US THE 365-DAY YEAR

If you've ever been annoyed by February's weird number of days, blame the Romans. Their calendar ran on a 355-day year with random extra months added by priests who used them for political gain.

Julius Caesar introduced the Julian calendar in 46 BC, adding extra days to reach 365. His astronomers miscalculated the actual solar year by 11 minutes, leading to centuries of drift.

Pope Gregory XIII fixed it in 1582, giving us the Gregorian calendar. That's why we have leap years and why February got stuck being the oddball month.

A man ate a plane. Rubber ducks mapped the ocean. A melted candy bar changed how we cook. Pizza made it to space. Bubble wrap started as wallpaper. And February has Julius Caesar to thank for its identity crisis. Not a bad place to start.

CHAPTER TWO

WILD KINGDOM

THE OCEAN'S ULTIMATE QUICK-CHANGE ARTIST

I magine changing your skin color, texture, and pattern in less than a second. That's the octopus.

At the heart of this shapeshifting ability are chromatophores, tiny sacs of pigment controlled by the octopus's nervous system. By expanding or contracting these sacs, octopuses can flash a new color instantly, from deep-sea black to neon yellow. But the real showstopper? They don't just change color. They change texture. Using muscle-controlled papillae, an octopus can morph from smooth to spiky in an instant, mimicking coral, sand, or even another creature.

Camouflage isn't just for survival. It's a full-blown language. Octopuses flash patterns to intimidate rivals, display waves to attract mates, and imitate other marine creatures to avoid predators. The mimic octopus can impersonate venomous sea snakes, lionfish, and jellyfish just by rearranging its body and colors.

The wildest part? Octopuses can match their surroundings without even using their eyes. Their skin has light-sensitive cells that do the work independently. Scientists are studying this to develop next-generation camouflage materials.

THE SLOTH: NATURE'S SLOW-MOTION GENIUS

If there were an Olympic event for moving as little as possible, sloths would take home the gold. Very slowly. These tree-dwelling mammals spend 90% of their lives hanging upside down, move at an average speed of 0.03 mph, and are so slow that algae literally grow on their fur, turning them into walking green ecosystems.

Don't mistake their lack of urgency for laziness. Sloths have mastered energy efficiency, surviving on nutritionally useless leaves that take up to a month to digest. Their metabolism is so slow that they only go to the bathroom once a week, and when they do, they risk getting eaten by predators. Coming down from the trees is their most dangerous moment.

It gets weirder. Sloths can hold their breath for 40 minutes, slowing their heart rate by a third. Some have been mistaken for floating corpses in rivers. They also have extra neck vertebrae, letting them turn their heads almost 270 degrees without moving their bodies.

Sloths are expert survivalists, using camouflage, patience, and sheer stubbornness to outlive faster predators. In the rainforest, slowness survives.

THE FISH THAT WALKS (AND FIGHTS) ON LAND

Meet the mudskipper, a fish that doesn't just survive on land. It thrives there. Unlike other fish, mudskippers hop, climb, and throw down in territorial battles, all while breathing air.

Mudskippers have modified pectoral fins that act like tiny legs, allowing them to shuffle, jump, and run across mud. They also have specially evolved gill chambers that trap water like an oxygen tank, letting them breathe out of water for hours. Some species even climb trees, using their fins as makeshift grappling hooks.

Lungfish take things further. These prehistoric fish have primitive lungs, allowing them to survive for months on land. When their watery homes dry up, they burrow into mud, coat themselves in mucus, and hibernate until rain returns.

These fish are proof of evolution in action. Scientists believe mudskippers and lungfish mirror the first fish that crawled onto land 375 million years ago, eventually evolving into amphibians, reptiles, and millions of years later, us.

THE BIRD THAT SEES COLORS YOU CAN'T EVEN IMAGINE

Your world is missing colors. A lot of them. While humans see red, green, and blue, birds experience an entire hidden spectrum, including ultraviolet light. To them, the sky isn't just blue. It's bursting with shades we'll never perceive.

Take the zebra finch. To us, males and females look nearly identical, but under UV light, their feathers reveal everything from health to social status. Birds use these hidden hues for finding mates, spotting ripe berries, and detecting predators.

If you've ever thought a peacock's feathers were dazzling, imagine what they look like to another peacock. Many birds flash UV signals as a kind of invisible language, a color-coded communication system we'll never see.

Scientists have tried simulating bird vision with computer models. The results are staggering. Birds see millions more shades than humans can comprehend. Compared to them, we're practically color-blind.

THE JELLYFISH THAT CAN LIVE FOREVER

Meet Turritopsis dohrnii, the only known biologically immortal animal on Earth.

When faced with stress, starvation, injury, or old age, this jellyfish transforms back into a baby and begins life all over again. It can repeat the process indefinitely.

Scientists call it transdifferentiation, a rare process where cells completely change type, reverting to their earliest forms. Many jellyfish still get eaten, so populations aren't exactly exploding. But some individuals could theoretically live forever.

Researchers are now studying whether this jellyfish holds clues to slowing aging in humans. Turritopsis dohrnii has been keeping that secret for over 500 million years.

THE SHRIMP THAT PUNCHES WITH THE POWER OF A BULLET

The mantis shrimp measures just a few inches long. It also has one of the fastest and most powerful punches in the animal kingdom.

A mantis shrimp can punch with the force of a .22-caliber bullet, moving at 50 mph in less than three milliseconds. The impact is so intense it boils the water around it, creating tiny plasma explosions called cavitation bubbles. Even if the punch doesn't kill its prey, the shockwave from the bubble collapse delivers a second hit.

Mantis shrimp use this to crack open crabs, clams, and aquarium glass. They've shattered tanks. They also have some of the most advanced eyes in the animal kingdom, capable of seeing polarized light and 16 types of color receptors. Humans have three.

From color-changing octopuses to immortal jellyfish, sloths that get mistaken for floating corpses, and a shrimp that shatters glass with its fist. Nature didn't need to go this hard. It did anyway.

CHAPTER THREE

THE SPORTS SECTION

THE BASEBALL PLAYER WHO WAS TRADED FOR A BAG OF BATS

Most baseball trades involve big money and star players. Not this one.

In 2008, John Odom, a right-handed pitcher in the independent minor leagues, was set to join the Calgary Vipers. When visa issues prevented him from playing in Canada, his original team, the Laredo Broncos, needed a quick solution. They traded Odom to the Redding Colts in exchange for ten maple baseball bats, valued at $665.

Odom took it in stride, joking that he was now "part wood." He even considered the nickname "Bat Man." The trade made headlines worldwide and turned him into a cult figure.

Odom passed away later that year, struggling with personal issues. His baseball career was short. But he's remembered, just not for strikeouts.

THE LONGEST TENNIS MATCH BROKE THE SCOREBOARD

No one expected John Isner and Nicolas Mahut's 2010 Wimbledon match to last 11 hours and 5 minutes across three days. The final set alone ran 8 hours. Fans came and went, commentators ran out of things to say, and the electronic scoreboard broke down. It wasn't built for a score like 70-68.

Isner eventually won. Both players were spent. Wimbledon later introduced a rule change to make sure it never happened again.

They were playing a first-round match.

THE TOUR DE FRANCE USED TO ALLOW RIDERS TO DRINK BEER MID-RACE

In the early 1900s, Tour de France cyclists refueled with beer, wine, and champagne during the race. Riders stopped at roadside bars or had team assistants hand them bottles mid-ride. Alcohol was thought to relieve pain, boost endurance, and act as a stimulant.

It wasn't until the 1960s that sports scientists confirmed it was doing the opposite. Alcohol dehydrates, slows reaction time, and impairs muscle function. Officials eventually banned it, and cyclists switched to water, energy gels, and recovery shakes.

For a brief and glorious window, though, beer was race fuel.

THE U.S. WOMEN'S SOCCER TEAM'S 13-0 BLOWOUT

Soccer is a game of tight, low-scoring battles. Not on June 11, 2019.

The U.S. Women's National Team faced Thailand in the group stage of the FIFA Women's World Cup and won 13-0. The biggest blowout in World Cup history, men's or women's. The U.S. scored an average of one goal every six minutes. Alex Morgan alone put away five, tying the World Cup record for most goals in a single game.

The victory sparked debate. Some argued the excessive celebrations were unsportsmanlike. Others said it's the World Cup. You play your best.

The record still stands.

THE WOMAN WHO SWAM FROM CUBA TO FLORIDA WITHOUT A CAGE

In 2013, at age 64, Diana Nyad became the first person to swim from Cuba to Florida without a shark cage. 110 miles of open ocean, surrounded by sharks, jellyfish, and unpredictable currents. She had been attempting it for 35 years.

After five failed attempts, she completed the 53-hour swim. She battled dehydration, exhaustion, hallucinations, and deadly box jellyfish stings that had nearly ended previous tries. This time she came prepared. A silicone mask protected her from jellyfish, and her team used electronic shark deterrents.

When she reached the Florida shore she told the crowd: "Never, ever give up."

THE GOLFER WHO HIT THE SAME BALL FOR OVER 5 HOURS

In 1961, Moe Norman played an entire round of golf using one ball, not on a course but across an entire Canadian province. Over five hours, he hit the same ball more than 400 miles.

Norman was an eccentric golf legend, known for a near-perfect swing and unconventional methods. He once hit 1,500 balls in a single day for fun. Fellow golfers said he could land a ball on a handkerchief from 200 yards away.

The 400-mile, one-ball day fits him perfectly.

A traded pitcher, a tennis match that broke the scoreboard, cyclists drinking beer mid-race, a 13-0 demolition, a 64-year-old swimming through sharks, and a man who hit a golf ball across a province. Sports, it turns out, have very little to do with the rulebook.

CHAPTER FOUR

HIDDEN SECRETS OF FAMOUS LANDMARKS

THE ABANDONED CITY BENEATH LAS VEGAS

L as Vegas is known for glitz, glamour, and flashing neon lights. Beneath it is something else entirely.

The city's storm drain system stretches over 600 miles, forming a vast tunnel network under the Strip. Built to prevent flash floods, these tunnels have since become home to hundreds of people, an underground community known as "The Mole People." Many ended up there through financial hardship, addiction, or personal struggle.

These spaces are equipped with furniture, bookshelves, and electricity tapped from streetlights. Some residents have lived there for years, forming their own community in the dark beneath one of the most expensive stretches of real estate in the world.

THE EIFFEL TOWER HAS A SECRET APARTMENT AT THE TOP

Gustave Eiffel built a private apartment for himself at the top of his tower. Most of the millions who visit every year have no idea it's there.

The space was furnished with plush armchairs, wooden cabinets, patterned wallpaper, and a grand piano. Eiffel didn't use it for parties. It was a quiet place to work. Occasionally he brought guests, including Thomas Edison, who came to demonstrate his latest inventions.

Visitors today can peek inside through a small window.

MOUNT RUSHMORE HAS A HIDDEN ROOM BEHIND LINCOLN'S HEAD

Mount Rushmore isn't just four faces carved into a mountain. There's a secret chamber inside.

Sculptor Gutzon Borglum designed the Hall of Records to hold important documents, including the Declaration of Independence and the U.S. Constitution. Funding ran out before it was finished, and the chamber was sealed.

In 1998, the U.S. government placed historical documents inside, encased in titanium vaults. The chamber also contains a message for whoever discovers it centuries from now. It's in an area inaccessible to the public. Almost no one has seen it.

Borglum's original vision was grander. He wanted busts of famous Americans and a detailed account of the nation's history. That never happened. But the room is there, behind Lincoln's head, while tourists take selfies out front.

DISNEY WORLD HAS AN ENTIRE UNDERGROUND CITY

Beneath Disney World runs a massive tunnel system called the Utilidors. Most visitors have no idea it exists.

The tunnels allow cast members to move between attractions unseen, access staff areas, and use services like cafeterias and costume departments. There's also a high-tech garbage system that sucks trash through underground pipes, keeping the park clean without a single trash truck in sight.

Walt Disney built it after seeing a Frontierland cowboy walking through futuristic Tomorrowland. It broke the illusion. His solution was an entire underground city.

THE EMPIRE STATE BUILDING HAS A FAKE FLOOR

The Empire State Building soars 102 stories above New York City. Except not all of those floors are real.

Between the 86th-floor observation deck and the building's actual top, several levels exist only on paper. The phantom floors were designed with extra-high ceilings to make the skyscraper appear taller, helping it claim the title of world's tallest building when it opened in 1931. The Chrysler Building had briefly held that title. The extra floors settled it.

These hidden floors are mostly inaccessible, housing mechanical equipment or just empty space. Some are tall enough to be split into multiple levels. The Empire State Building is no longer the world's tallest, but the trick worked.

THE GREAT PYRAMID OF GIZA HAS A HIDDEN CHAMBER

For thousands of years, the Great Pyramid was believed to be fully explored. In 2017, scientists found a 100-foot-long void above the Grand Gallery using advanced scanning technology.

Nobody knows what's inside. Theories range from a hidden burial chamber to lost artifacts to architectural supports. The pyramid's structure makes it too delicate to access yet.

The Great Pyramid is 4,500 years old and still has secrets.

Secret apartments, underground cities, phantom floors, a hidden room behind Lincoln's head, and a pyramid that still hasn't shown us everything. The most visited places in the world are apparently very good at keeping quiet.

CHAPTER FIVE

THE STRANGEST THINGS
EVER SENT INTO SPACE

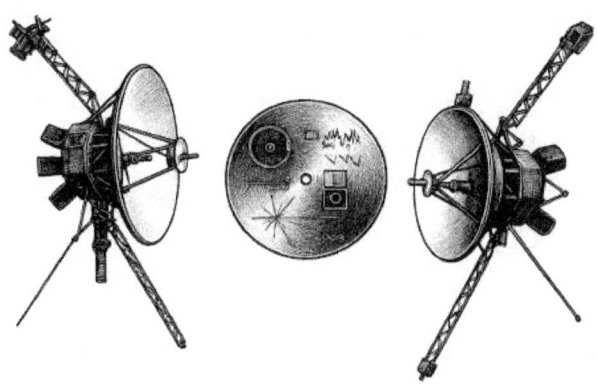

NASA SENT A GOLDEN RECORD MEANT FOR ALIENS

In 1977, NASA launched Voyager 1 and 2 to explore the outer solar system. They didn't just carry cameras and sensors. They carried a message.

Each probe included a 12-inch golden record packed with audio recordings, music, and greetings in 55 languages. Waves, laughter, babies crying, a message from the U.N. Secretary General. The idea was to help aliens find us.

Both Voyagers are now drifting through interstellar space. Somewhere out there, Chuck Berry's 'Johnny B. Goode' is still traveling.

NASA SENT TARDIGRADES INTO SPACE

Tardigrades are microscopic eight-legged creatures, also known as water bears. They are almost certainly the toughest animals on Earth, and possibly anywhere else.

In 2007, scientists sent a group into low-Earth orbit aboard a European Space Agency mission. The tardigrades were exposed to the vacuum of space, cosmic radiation, and extreme temperatures. No spacesuit. They survived. Some came home and reproduced.

They are now top candidates for biological research in space. If life ever needs to survive on Mars or the Moon, the water bear has already done the homework.

NASA SENT LEGO FIGURINES TO JUPITER

NASA's Juno spacecraft, currently orbiting Jupiter, is carrying three tiny LEGO astronauts on a 1.7-billion-mile journey.

In 2011, NASA teamed up with LEGO to send custom aluminum minifigures of Galileo, Jupiter, and Juno into deep space. The goal was to inspire kids about space exploration.

They are still out there, orbiting Jupiter right now.

If aliens ever find the Juno spacecraft, they may conclude Earth is ruled by tiny indestructible plastic people.

NASA Is Trying to Grow a Garden in Space

If humans want to live on Mars, we need to figure out how to grow food first. NASA has been working on it.

In 2015, astronauts aboard the International Space Station grew and ate space lettuce for the first time. Since then they've experimented with radishes, wheat, and chili peppers, all in zero gravity.

The challenge is water. Without gravity it doesn't flow downward, making soil farming impossible. Astronauts use hydroponics, LED grow lights, and nutrient-infused mist instead.

Freeze-dried food will only get us so far.

Space Whiskey: Scientists Aged Scotch in Zero Gravity

In 2011, the Ardbeg Distillery sent whiskey to the International Space Station to see how zero gravity would change its aging process. It spent nearly three years orbiting Earth.

When it came back, experts compared it to a batch aged under normal conditions. Space whiskey tasted completely different. Flavor notes included "intensely woody, with notes of antiseptic smoke and rubbery bacon."

Not a smooth sip. But an interesting one.

The Salmon That Became an Astronaut

In 1973, NASA sent a live salmon to space aboard Skylab, America's first space station. Scientists wanted to see if fish could navigate without gravity.

At first the salmon was completely confused, flailing and spinning. After a few days it figured out a new way to swim.

The experiment helped researchers understand how weightlessness affects the brain and movement, useful data for planning future space travel.

The salmon adapted. That's the whole story.

A golden record, three LEGO figurines, a confused salmon, space lettuce, and whiskey that tastes like rubbery bacon. We are a very specific kind of civilization.

CHAPTER SIX

AWES OF ARCHITECTURE

THE LEANING TOWER OF PISA WAS NEVER MEANT TO LEAN

Construction began in 1173, and after just five years, builders noticed the tower was sinking on one side. They had built it on soft, unstable ground.

For centuries, engineers tried to fix it. Every attempt made things worse. By the 1990s the tilt was so extreme that experts feared collapse. After major restoration efforts they stabilized it, but it will never be straight.

The tilt has actually helped it survive earthquakes that destroyed nearby buildings. Its unusual center of gravity lets it absorb tremors that would topple a straight structure. Experts believe it will stand for at least another 200 years.

An engineering disaster became one of the most recognizable landmarks in the world.

A SKYSCRAPER IN LONDON ACCIDENTALLY MELTED CARS

In 2013, London unveiled 20 Fenchurch Street, a curved glass skyscraper locals nicknamed "The Walkie-Talkie." It quickly earned a second nickname: "The Walkie-Scorchie."

The building's concave glass facade acted like a giant magnifying glass, concentrating sunlight onto the street below. The reflected rays melted car parts, scorched pavement, and burned shopfronts. One Jaguar owner came back to find his side mirror, panels, and dashboard warped from the heat. Temperatures on the street reached over 196°F in some spots.

Engineers eventually installed sunshades and a protective film to diffuse the light.

The building is still standing. They just had to stop it from cooking the neighborhood.

THE COLOSSEUM WAS COVERED IN MARBLE UNTIL IT WAS STOLEN

When the Colosseum was built in 80 AD, it wasn't a crumbling ruin. It was covered in white marble, one of the most impressive structures of its time.

Then people stole it.

After the fall of the Roman Empire, builders looted the marble to construct churches, palaces, and buildings across Rome. St. Peter's Basilica contains marble that was once part of the Colosseum.

Rome recycled itself.

SEATTLE BUILT A FAKE CITY ON TOP OF A FACTORY TO TRICK ENEMY BOMBERS

During World War II, Seattle's Boeing aircraft plant was a prime target for enemy bombers. The government's solution was to build an entire fake city on top of it.

Using wood, canvas, netting, and wire, workers constructed fake houses, streets, trees, parked cars, clotheslines with laundry, and painted sidewalks. From the air it looked like a quiet suburban neighborhood.

It worked. Seattle was never bombed. The Boeing plant kept producing aircraft. After the war the fake city was dismantled.

THE GATEWAY ARCH MOVES WITH THE WIND

The Gateway Arch in St. Louis stands 630 feet tall, the tallest monument in the U.S. It also sways.

Because of its curved, hollow design, the arch can move up to 18 inches in either direction without breaking. Engineers built it that way to withstand wind and earthquakes.

Visitors ride a tram to the top. On windy days, they can feel it move.

THE GOLDEN BRIDGE IN VIETNAM LOOKS LIKE IT'S HELD UP BY GIANT HANDS

In Vietnam's Ba Na Hills, the Golden Bridge appears to be lifted by two enormous stone hands. The design is intentional, meant to look like gods helping humans cross between worlds.

The bridge sits about 4,600 feet above sea level and stretches roughly 490 feet long. The hands aren't stone at all. They're fiberglass and wire mesh, built to look ancient and weathered.

It was built in 2018. It is now one of the most photographed landmarks in the world.

Marble looted for cathedrals, a factory hidden under a fake neighborhood, a monument that sways in the wind, and a bridge held up by giant stone hands. Architecture has a much stranger resume than most people realize.

CHAPTER SEVEN

IT'S IN THE WRITING

DID HEMINGWAY REALLY WRITE A SIX-WORD STORY?

"For sale: baby shoes, never worn."

This famous six-word story has long been credited to Ernest Hemingway, supposedly written on a challenge. It sparked an entire genre of flash fiction and inspired countless writers to explore ultra-short storytelling.

But he probably didn't write it.

There's no documented proof Hemingway ever wrote it. The first known mention of the anecdote appeared in the 1990s, decades after his death in 1961. Some researchers believe it's an urban legend. Others trace similar six-word ads to the early 1900s, before Hemingway's time. Short, tragic classified ads were a common device in early 20th century newspapers.

The attribution persists because it fits his style. But the origin is almost certainly not him.

DR. SEUSS WROTE GREEN EGGS AND HAM ON A BET

After the success of The Cat in the Hat, Dr. Seuss's publisher Bennett Cerf bet him $50 he couldn't write a book using 50 words or fewer. Seuss took the bet. The result was Green Eggs and Ham.

He used exactly 50 different words, repeated in creative combinations to build rhythm, humor, and a stubborn little character who absolutely will not try green eggs and ham. In a boat, with a goat, in the rain, on a train. The repetition wasn't just fun. It turned out to be genuinely useful for early readers building vocabulary and confidence.

The book became his best-selling work, with over 8 million copies sold worldwide. It has outlasted almost everything else in children's literature and eventually became a Netflix series.

Cerf never collected.

MARY SHELLEY WROTE FRANKENSTEIN BECAUSE OF A BET

One of the greatest horror novels ever written started as a party game.

In 1816, Mary Shelley, her husband Percy Shelley, and the poet Lord Byron were stuck inside during a stormy summer at Lake

Geneva. Bored and restless, Byron challenged everyone to write a ghost story. That night, Shelley had a terrifying dream of a scientist creating a monstrous, reanimated corpse. She woke up and started writing.

She was 18 years old. The first draft became Frankenstein, one of the most enduring horror novels in history. Not bad for a rainy night with nothing to do.

SHAKESPEARE INVENTED OVER 1,700 WORDS WE USE TODAY

William Shakespeare didn't just write some of the most famous plays in history. He also invented over 1,700 words that we still use today.

If you've ever used "bedazzled," "swagger," "gloomy," "addiction," "laughable," or "fashionable," you can thank Shakespeare. He had a knack for bending language to fit his creative needs. He turned nouns into verbs, like "elbow." He mashed words together, like "new-fangled." He crafted terms out of thin air, like "unreal."

English in the late 1500s and early 1600s was still evolving, and Shakespeare had a front-row seat in shaping it. His expanded vocabulary made his plays richer and more expressive, adding layers of meaning that audiences hadn't heard before.

His impact on the English language is, in his own word, monumental.

VICTOR HUGO WROTE A SENTENCE THAT'S 823 WORDS LONG

Victor Hugo, author of Les Misérables, was not known for keeping things short. But even by his standards, one sentence stands out. It runs 823 words without a single period, sprawling across multiple pages and covering politics, philosophy, and revolution in one long, breathless thought.

Hugo wasn't alone in his love of the epic sentence. James Joyce, Marcel Proust, and William Faulkner all wrote infamously long passages. But 823 words is a different category entirely.

Anyone who has ever complained about a long text message has no idea what they're talking about.

THE SECRET LIBRARIES HIDDEN FROM THE NAZIS

During World War II, books became just as dangerous as weapons.

Inside the Warsaw Ghetto, Jewish residents secretly operated an underground library while facing starvation, disease, and daily threats of execution. The library was hidden inside a disguised building and contained thousands of books smuggled in by resistance members. Students, teachers, and intellectuals risked their lives to keep it running, believing that as long as books survived, something essential survived with them.

Across Europe, similar libraries were hidden in cellars, churches, and tucked under Nazi officers' noses. The effort wasn't just about preserving paper. It was a deliberate act of resistance, a refusal to let an entire culture be erased.

A bet produced Frankenstein. Another produced Green Eggs and Ham. A man wrote 823 words without stopping. And somewhere in Warsaw, people hid books from soldiers with guns. Literature has always been stranger and tougher than it looks.

CHAPTER EIGHT

CLASSICAL MUSIC ISN'T ALWAYS PEACEFUL

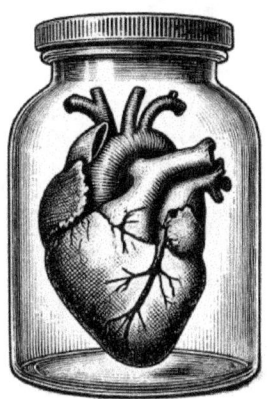

CHOPIN'S HEART WAS SMUGGLED INTO POLAND IN A JAR

Before he died, Frédéric Chopin had one final request: that his heart be removed and taken back to Poland.

In 1849, the legendary composer died in Paris, far from his homeland. His sister honored the wish in the most dramatic way possible. She had his heart cut from his body, sealed in a jar of cognac, and secretly smuggled across the border into Poland.

For over a century, Chopin's heart was kept hidden inside a church pillar in Warsaw, surviving wars, revolutions, and Nazi occupation. In 2014, researchers were finally allowed to examine it. The heart was perfectly preserved and showed signs of tuberculosis, the disease that likely killed him.

He died in France. His heart never left Poland.

Beethoven Composed Some of His Greatest Works While Completely Deaf

By his late 20s, Beethoven was losing his hearing. By his 40s, he was almost completely deaf. He composed some of his greatest work anyway.

His Ninth Symphony, featuring the famous "Ode to Joy," was written during this period. He could still hear music in his head, and he used vibrations to feel sound physically. He sawed the legs off his piano so he could press his ear to the floor and feel the notes through the wood.

At the premiere of the Ninth Symphony, Beethoven couldn't hear the applause. When he finally turned around, he saw the entire audience on their feet, cheering and waving. Some of the musicians wept.

Mozart Had a Bizarre Sense of Humor

Mozart wasn't just a musical genius. He also had the humor of a 12-year-old.

He loved crude jokes, pranks, and ridiculous letters. He composed an entire piece titled "Leck mich im Arsch," which translates from German exactly as badly as you think it does. The lyrics were originally a joke between friends. He also sent letters full of bathroom humor, wrote silly rhymes about bodily functions, and gave his pet starling a proper funeral when it died.

His music was some of the most sophisticated ever written. His jokes absolutely were not.

Bach Was Once Arrested for Trying to Quit His Job

In 1717, Bach wanted to leave his position as court musician for the Duke of Weimar to take a better job elsewhere. When he submitted his resignation, the Duke didn't just refuse. He threw Bach in jail.

Bach spent nearly a month behind bars for trying to quit. He used the time to compose new music.

Eventually the Duke let him go. Bach took the job.

The Greatest Musical Duel That Never Happened

Bach and Handel were two of the greatest composers of their era, born just 80 miles apart in Germany. They never once met.

Bach tried multiple times. The most famous near-miss came when Handel was visiting Halle, Bach's home region. Bach rushed to find him. By the time he arrived, Handel had already left.

Some historians think Handel deliberately avoided the meeting. Others chalk it up to bad timing. Either way, the closest thing to a musical showdown the Baroque era had to offer never happened.

VIVALDI WAS A PRIEST UNTIL HE DITCHED CHURCH FOR MUSIC

Antonio Vivaldi, the composer behind The Four Seasons, was ordained as a priest in 1703. He was known as "The Red Priest" for his bright red hair. He was less known for showing up to Mass.

His excuse was asthma. It made delivering sermons too difficult. Somehow it did not prevent him from composing and conducting orchestras.

Eventually he stopped pretending and devoted himself entirely to music, becoming one of the defining composers of the Baroque era.

THE ORCHESTRA THAT PLAYED UNTIL THE END

As the Titanic sank on April 15, 1912, a group of eight musicians led by violinist Wallace Hartley kept playing.

They started with lively tunes to keep passengers calm. As the situation worsened, they shifted to hymns. Most survivors recalled the last piece as "Nearer, My God, to Thee," though some accounts suggest it was a waltz called "Autumn." None of the band members survived.

Hartley's violin was strapped to his body when it was recovered from the ocean. It was later authenticated and sold at auction for $1.7 million, making it the most expensive Titanic artifact ever sold. A statue of Hartley stands in his English hometown today.

They knew what was happening. They played anyway.

A smuggled heart, a composer jailed for quitting, a priest who skipped Mass to write concertos, a near-miss between the two greatest musicians of an era, and a band that played while a ship went down. Classical music had no shortage of drama.

CHAPTER NINE

REAL-LIFE HEISTS THAT SOUND LIKE MOVIES

THE ELDERLY GANG THAT MADE A ROOKIE MISTAKE

In 2015, a group of elderly criminals nicknamed "The Bad Grandpas" broke into the Hatton Garden Safe Deposit vault in London and stole over $20 million in cash, jewelry, and gold bars. Their ages ranged from 58 to 76. Some used hearing aids.

Over Easter weekend, they drilled through two feet of concrete, disabled alarms, and methodically emptied safety deposit boxes. For a while it looked like they had gotten away with it.

Then gang member Danny Jones started bragging. He sent text messages to associates about the loot, leading investigators straight to him. Other members kept returning to their hiding spot, drawing attention. When police finally moved in, the getaway van was still full of jewelry and cash.

Decades of experience. One very avoidable mistake.

THE LEGO THIEVES WHO STOLE MILLIONS IN TOY BRICKS

Between 2019 and 2021, an organized gang traveled across France, Poland, and Germany stealing thousands of Lego sets from toy stores. Their targets were rare collections, particularly Star Wars and Harry Potter sets, which can sell for thousands on the black market.

The operation grew large enough to support dedicated Lego resale networks. When authorities caught them, they found an entire warehouse full of stolen sets.

Somewhere out there, a criminal enterprise was built entirely out of toy bricks.

THE CRIMINALS WHO POSED AS COPS TO ROB A BANK

In Brazil's biggest bank heist, a gang spent three months digging a 260-foot tunnel under the Banco Central in Fortaleza. When they broke through into the vault, they dressed as police officers, walked in, and left with seven tons of cash. $70 million total. No alarms.

Authorities didn't realize the money was gone until the next business day. When they investigated, they found an empty vault and a perfectly engineered tunnel.

Most of the money was never recovered. Some of the robbers were never found.

THE MONA LISA WAS ONCE STOLEN BY A MUSEUM WORKER

In 1911, a thief walked into the Louvre, took the Mona Lisa off the wall, and left.

His name was Vincenzo Peruggia, an Italian handyman who had worked at the museum. Convinced the painting belonged in Italy, he hid inside the Louvre overnight, waited until it closed, then walked out the next morning dressed like a worker with the painting tucked under his coat.

The Mona Lisa was missing for two years. Police were baffled. Pablo Picasso was questioned as a suspect. In 1913, Peruggia was caught trying to sell it to an art dealer in Italy.

He served seven months. In Italy, he was treated as a folk hero. The heist made the Mona Lisa the most famous painting in the world, which it arguably wasn't before someone stole it.

THE LUFTHANSA HEIST THAT INSPIRED GOODFELLAS

In 1978, a crew led by mobster Jimmy Burke stole $5 million in cash and $1 million in jewels from a high-security vault at JFK Airport. They had inside information from a Lufthansa employee who knew when untraceable European cash would be stored there. The plan was straightforward: storm the vault, tie up the employees, grab the money, disappear.

It worked. Within an hour they had what amounts to $25 million in today's money.

Then the crew started disappearing, eliminated one by one by Burke himself, who feared they'd talk. Much of the money was never recovered. Burke, the real-life inspiration for Robert De Niro's character in Goodfellas, took most of the secrets with him when he died.

THE GARDNER MUSEUM HEIST: A $500 MILLION MYSTERY

In 1990, two thieves dressed as Boston police officers knocked on the door of the Isabella Stewart Gardner Museum and told the guards they were responding to a disturbance. The guards let them in. The thieves handcuffed them, locked them in the basement, and spent 81 minutes stealing $500 million worth of art.

Among the stolen pieces were Rembrandt's Storm on the Sea of Galilee, Vermeer's The Concert, and a rare Degas sketch.

Not one painting has been recovered. The FBI believes organized crime was behind it, but the thieves have never been identified. The museum still keeps the empty frames on the walls.

That was over 30 years ago.

A tunnel under a Brazilian bank, a handyman walking out of the Louvre, elderly thieves with a van full of evidence, and $500 million in paintings still hanging somewhere unknown. The empty frames at the Gardner Museum have been waiting for 30 years. They're still waiting.

CHAPTER TEN

UNBELIEVABLE
UNSOLVED MYSTERIES

THE "WOW!" SIGNAL: A POSSIBLE MESSAGE FROM ALIENS?

In 1977, a scientist at Ohio State University's "Big Ear" radio telescope picked up a mysterious deep-space radio signal. It was so shocking that he circled the data and wrote "Wow!" in the margins.

The signal lasted 72 seconds, was 30 times stronger than normal background noise, and came from the direction of the constellation Sagittarius. Scientists ruled out airplanes, satellites, and natural space phenomena. The signal's origin remains a total mystery.

Did aliens send it? No one knows. Despite decades of searching, the "Wow!" signal was never detected again.

THE GHOST SHIP MARY CELESTE: A CREW THAT VANISHED WITHOUT A TRACE

In 1872, sailors aboard the ship Dei Gratia spotted a mysterious vessel drifting aimlessly in the Atlantic Ocean. As they approached, they realized it was the Mary Celeste, a ship that had set sail eight days earlier.

Everything on board was perfectly intact: cargo, supplies, and even a sailor's half-eaten breakfast. The only thing missing? The entire crew.

There was no sign of a struggle, no distress signals, and the lifeboat was gone. Why would trained sailors abandon a perfectly seaworthy ship in the middle of the ocean?

Theories range from pirates, mutiny, and freak weather events to poisonous fumes from alcohol barrels causing mass hysteria. Despite 150 years of speculation, nobody knows what happened to them.

THE GREEN CHILDREN OF WOOLPIT: A MEDICAL MYSTERY

In the 12th century, villagers in Woolpit, England, discovered two young children wandering near a pit. They had green skin and spoke an unknown language.

The children, a boy and a girl, refused to eat anything except raw beans. Over time, they adapted to normal food, and their skin slowly lost its green tint. The boy died shortly after their discovery, but the girl grew up and learned to speak English, revealing a bizarre story:

She claimed they came from a place with no sun, where everything was twilight and green. She called it "St. Martin's Land" and said they had been herding cattle when they suddenly found themselves in Woolpit.

Theories about their origins range from malnourished orphans suffering from chlorosis (a condition causing green-tinged skin) to interdimensional travelers or extraterrestrials. Over 800 years later, no one knows where the Green Children came from. Or if they were even human.

THE ZODIAC KILLER'S CIPHERS: THE CODES THAT STILL HAVEN'T BEEN CRACKED

The Zodiac Killer is one of the most infamous serial killers in history, taunting police with mysterious letters and cryptic ciphers, some of which remain unsolved to this day.

During the late 1960s, the Zodiac terrorized Northern California, sending coded messages to newspapers alongside gruesome confessions. One cipher was cracked in 2020, revealing a chilling message: "I hope you are having lots of fun in trying to catch me."

The "340-character cipher" and "Z13 cipher," which supposedly contains his real name, have never been solved. Cryptographers, codebreakers, and the FBI have all tried.

Did he really leave behind his name? Or was it all part of one last, unsolvable game?

THE DYATLOV PASS INCIDENT: NINE HIKERS WHO DIED UNDER BIZARRE CIRCUMSTANCES

In 1959, nine experienced hikers set off on a trek in the Ural Mountains of Soviet Russia. None of them made it back.

Their tent was discovered ripped open from the inside, as if they had fled in terror. Footprints led away into the snow, some barefoot despite subzero temperatures. The bodies were found miles away, some with severe internal injuries, crushed ribs, and fractured skulls, with no external wounds. One hiker was missing her tongue and eyes. Traces of radiation were found on some of their clothing.

Theories range from a secret military experiment gone wrong to an avalanche to infrasound waves triggering mass panic. Some claim a yeti or aliens were involved. No definitive explanation has ever been found.

THE DISAPPEARANCE OF FLIGHT MH370: A PLANE THAT VANISHED WITHOUT A TRACE

On March 8, 2014, Malaysia Airlines Flight MH370 took off from Kuala Lumpur, bound for Beijing with 239 passengers and crew. It never arrived.

About 40 minutes into the flight, MH370's transponders shut off and the plane vanished from radar. It then made a mysterious turn westward, flew off course for several more hours, and was never seen again.

Search teams combed the Indian Ocean for years, spending over $160 million in the largest and most expensive search operation in aviation history. A few fragments washed up on distant shores. The main wreckage and black box were never found.

Theories range from mechanical failure and pilot suicide to hijacking and secret military intervention. Some believe it was deliberately taken off course. Others think it was shot down.

Nobody knows.

A crew walked off a seaworthy ship. Nine hikers fled their own tent in the dark. A plane carrying 239 people disappeared mid-flight. A serial killer may have spelled out his name in code, and nobody can read it. Some of these cases are over a century old. None of them are closed.

CHAPTER ELEVEN

CAUTION! DANGER AHEAD!

SNAKE ISLAND: A PLACE SO DEADLY, IT'S ILLEGAL TO VISIT

Imagine stepping onto an island where there's one deadly snake per square meter. That's exactly why Ilha da Queimada Grande, better known as Snake Island, is one of the most dangerous places on Earth, and why the Brazilian government has banned visitors entirely.

This remote island, about 90 miles off Brazil's coast, is the only natural home of the critically endangered golden lancehead viper. Trapped there thousands of years ago when rising ocean levels cut the island off from the mainland, these vipers adapted in isolation, evolving an insanely potent venom that can melt flesh. With no natural predators to keep them in check, their population exploded.

According to legend, the island was once inhabited, but the last lighthouse keeper and his family met a gruesome fate at the fangs of these snakes in the 1920s. Today, Queimada Grande is strictly off-limits, not just to protect people, but to preserve the vipers. Only the Brazilian Navy and select researchers, vetted by the Chico Mendes Institute for Biodiversity Conservation, are allowed to visit, and even they need special permits and protective gear.

Good luck finding a boat willing to take you.

THE DOOR TO HELL: A CRATER THAT'S BEEN BURNING FOR 50+ YEARS

In the middle of Turkmenistan's Karakum Desert, there's a massive crater where flames rise from the ground day and night. Locals call it "The Door to Hell," and it's been burning nonstop since the 1970s.

This pit was created when Soviet geologists were drilling for natural gas and accidentally punched into a massive underground cavern. The ground collapsed, opening a 230-foot-wide hole. Fearing that toxic gas could escape, scientists lit it on fire, expecting it to burn out in a few days.

More than 50 years later, it's still burning. No one knows exactly how much gas is left, or when, or if, the fire will ever go out. The Turkmenistan government has tried multiple times to extinguish it, but the flames keep coming back.

THE BOLIVIAN "DEATH ROAD": THE MOST DANGEROUS DRIVE IN THE WORLD

Most roads have guardrails, traffic signs, and maybe a few potholes. Bolivia's Yungas Road, better known as "Death Road," has none of those things. Just a sheer drop of up to 2,000 feet with no second chances.

This 40-mile stretch winds through the Andes Mountains, twisting along narrow, fog-covered cliffs with barely enough room for one vehicle at a time. Until the early 2000s, it was the only route connecting La Paz to the Amazon rainforest, and it claimed the lives of 300 people per year.

Even today, despite a safer alternate route, thrill-seekers and mountain bikers flock to Death Road, testing their luck on a path where one wrong move means plummeting off the edge.

LAKE NATRON: THE WATER THAT TURNS ANIMALS TO "STONE"

In Tanzania, there's a lake so extreme it mummifies animals that touch it.

Lake Natron is one of the most inhospitable places on Earth. Its water is so alkaline it can reach a pH of 12, almost as caustic as ammonia or bleach. The lake's bizarre chemistry comes from volcanic minerals, which coat the surrounding landscape. When birds or bats accidentally crash into the water, their bodies become perfectly preserved, turning into eerie, stone-like sculptures.

Despite its hellish conditions, some life thrives here. Flamingos use the lake's shallow waters as a safe nesting ground, since the extreme alkalinity keeps predators away. A species of hardy fish has also adapted to survive in the salty, boiling-hot water.

The lake is toxic enough to mummify a bird on contact. The flamingos nested there anyway.

MOUNT EVEREST'S "DEATH ZONE": THE PLACE WHERE YOUR BODY STARTS DYING

Climbing Mount Everest is a bucket-list dream for many. Above 26,000 feet, it becomes a nightmare known as the "Death Zone."

At this altitude, oxygen levels are so low that the human body starts shutting down. Without supplemental oxygen, climbers experience hallucinations, brain swelling, and lungs filling with fluid. The lack of oxygen slows brain function, making even simple decisions life-threatening.

Everest is also littered with the frozen bodies of climbers who never made it back down. Recovering them is nearly impossible. Some serve as landmarks for future climbers.

There are over 200 bodies up there. Most of them are staying.

THE DEVIL'S POOL: SWIMMING AT THE EDGE OF A 350-FOOT WATERFALL

Most people wouldn't swim at the edge of a 350-foot waterfall. At Victoria Falls in Africa, thrill-seekers do it on purpose.

Known as "The Devil's Pool," this natural rock formation creates a small, relatively calm swimming area right at the edge of the world's largest waterfall. When water levels are low, between August and December, visitors can swim right up to the drop-off and look down at the falls below.

One wrong move and you're over the edge. The line for tickets is long.

Most of these places are still open for visitors. That's either reassuring or deeply alarming, depending on your vacation style.

CHAPTER TWELVE

THEY PAY YOU FOR THAT?

PROFESSIONAL PENGUIN BABYSITTER

If your dream job involves hanging out with adorable penguins all day, penguin babysitters exist.

In Antarctica, penguins are a protected species, and researchers studying them need human assistants to keep the little waddlers safe. These caretakers help monitor penguin colonies, protect them from environmental threats, and sometimes rescue lost chicks.

One major duty: preventing penguins from getting too curious. These birds are fearless and have a habit of wandering into research stations, stealing supplies, or pecking at expensive equipment. Some babysitters have to gently nudge them back to their nests, all while trying not to laugh at their clumsy antics.

It's cold, remote, and requires months of isolation. For penguin lovers, apparently worth it.

PROFESSIONAL DOG FOOD TASTER

Some people taste wine for a living. Others taste dog food.

Professional dog food tasters exist, and their job is exactly what it sounds like: sampling kibble and canned meat meant for man's best friend. Their mission is ensuring dog food has the right texture, aroma, and balance of flavors, because apparently dogs have standards.

Before dog food hits the shelves, tasters chew and analyze different brands, checking for flavor consistency and nutritional quality. They spit it out after tasting, but they still get the full meaty, grainy, occasionally fish-flavored experience.

Some tasters claim high-end dog food isn't that bad. A few brands apparently taste like pâté. Still not fine dining.

PROFESSIONAL ODOR JUDGE (A.K.A. SOMEONE WHO GETS PAID TO SMELL STUFF)

Ever wondered how companies decide if a deodorant actually works? Or how detergent brands prove their products make clothes smell "fresh"? That's where odor judges come in: people whose entire job is sniffing things and rating how good or bad they smell.

These professionals evaluate everything from perfumes to cleaning products to people's breath. Bad breath specialists exist too. Some smell armpits to test how well a deodorant holds up over time.

To qualify, you need an exceptionally sensitive nose and must pass rigorous smell tests to prove you can distinguish subtle scents. Some judges undergo nasal training to fine-tune their abilities.

Nobody said it was glamorous.

PROFESSIONAL PAINT WATCHER

Watching paint dry sounds like the most boring thing imaginable. For one man in the UK, it's a full-time job.

Paint researcher Keith Jackson spends his days watching different types of paint dry under various conditions. He studies how humidity, temperature, and ingredients affect drying time, making sure wall paints, road markings, and airplane coatings dry properly.

The wrong formula could lead to paint cracking, peeling, or drying too slowly, costing companies millions in repairs and product recalls.

Millions of dollars ride on whether a coat of paint cures correctly. Keith Jackson is the guy making sure it does.

PROFESSIONAL LINE STANDERS

Hate waiting in line? Some people make a living doing it for you.

Professional line standers get paid to camp out in queues for the latest iPhones, front-row concert tickets, or government services like DMV appointments. In major cities like New York and Washington, D.C., people will drop hundreds of dollars to hire someone to hold their spot for hours, sometimes days.

Some line standers have turned it into a full-time career, with seasonal surges during major product launches. Many never even see the event. They hand off their spot to the paying customer and move on to the next gig.

PROFESSIONAL MERMAID

For some, dressing up as a mermaid is a childhood dream. For others, it's a full-time job.

Professional mermaids perform at aquariums, resorts, live events, and underwater photography shoots, swimming in custom-made tails that can cost thousands of dollars. Some work as mermaid fitness instructors, teaching people how to swim like Ariel. Swimming with your legs bound together is harder than it looks.

It's also physically demanding. Mermaids train their lungs to hold their breath for minutes at a time, perfect their underwater choreography, and make swimming in a 30-pound tail look effortless. Some take freediving certification courses to perform for extended periods beneath the surface.

Mermaids are hired for luxury events, themed weddings, corporate parties, and children's hospital visits. Some have turned it into social media careers with millions of followers.

Someone out there is getting paid to smell armpits today. Probably right now. Meanwhile, a penguin babysitter is nudging a bird away from expensive equipment, and a mermaid is checking the weight of her tail before a corporate party. The job market is something else.

CHAPTER THIRTEEN

IS THAT WHAT YOU'RE WEARING?

SOCKS MADE OF . . . RADIUM?

In the early 1900s, people were obsessed with radium, the glowing element discovered by Marie Curie. It was believed to have health benefits, so companies put it in everything, including clothing.

Fashion brands sold radium-infused lingerie, face powders, and dresses that would glow in the dark. One company advertised "Radium Socks," claiming they would keep feet warm by stimulating circulation.

The problem: radium is highly radioactive. By the 1920s, factory workers who handled radium products began suffering from radiation poisoning, losing teeth, developing tumors, and, in some cases, glowing in the dark themselves.

Once the dangers were exposed, radioactive fashion disappeared. For a brief moment, people were literally wearing radiation in the name of style.

HIGH HEELS WERE ORIGINALLY MADE FOR MEN

High heels are a staple of women's fashion today, but they were originally designed for men, and not just for style.

In the 1600s, European aristocrats and soldiers wore high heels as a symbol of power and practicality. Persian cavalrymen were among the first to adopt them, using heels to secure their feet in stirrups while riding horses. When the trend spread to Europe, high heels became a fashion statement for wealthy men, particularly in France. The taller the heel, the more status you had.

No one loved heels more than King Louis XIV of France. He made red-soled heels exclusive to nobility. Christian Louboutin did not invent that move. Louis XIV's portraits show him towering in ornate heels, using fashion as a display of dominance.

By the 18th century, heels shifted into women's fashion and men abandoned them for more "practical" shoes.

Kings and cavalry wore them first. Just something to think about next time someone calls heels impractical.

CORSETS THAT LITERALLY RESHAPED BONES

Victorian women weren't just tightening their corsets for fashion. They were permanently changing their skeletons.

For centuries, corsets were designed to cinch the waist into an hourglass figure. In the 19th century, the trend went to the extreme. Some women had waists as small as 16 inches, about the size of a large grapefruit.

Doctors warned that tight lacing could compress organs, restrict breathing, and cause fainting. X-rays later revealed something worse: some Victorian women's ribcages had permanently changed shape, bending inward to match the contour of their corsets.

Yikes. Sometimes it is "pain before beauty."

WHY PURPLE WAS ONCE THE MOST EXPENSIVE COLOR

For much of history, wearing purple meant you were either royalty or extremely rich.

Before modern dyes, the only way to create purple fabric was by crushing thousands of tiny sea snails, specifically the murex snail found in the Mediterranean. The process was so labor-intensive that one pound of purple dye cost as much as gold.

Only emperors, kings, and nobles could afford it. In ancient Rome, Emperor Nero banned anyone but himself from wearing purple robes.

The monopoly on purple ended in 1856 when a teenage chemist named William Perkin accidentally discovered the first synthetic purple dye while trying to make malaria medication. Suddenly, purple was affordable for everyone. No snails required.

Perkin was eighteen when he figured it out. He retired at thirty-six. Not bad for a failed malaria experiment.

THE ACCIDENTAL CREATION OF CHANEL NO. 5

One of the most famous perfumes in the world was created by mistake.

In 1921, Coco Chanel hired Russian-French chemist Ernest Beaux to develop a new fragrance. He presented ten samples, numbered 1 through 10. When Chanel smelled sample No. 5, she knew instantly.

The twist: Beaux had accidentally added too much of a synthetic compound called aldehydes, which intensified the scent and gave it a quality that had never been smelled before.

Chanel launched No. 5 as the first perfume to break away from the floral-heavy scents of the time. It became an instant hit. Marilyn Monroe famously said she wore nothing but Chanel No. 5 to bed. It remains one of the best-selling perfumes in history.

HOW JEANS BECAME A SYMBOL OF REBELLION

Today, jeans are everywhere. In the 1950s, they were controversial enough to get you turned away at the door.

Originally designed as durable work pants for miners and labor-ers, jeans were practical but unfashionable until Hollywood changed everything. When James Dean wore them in Rebel Without a Cause and Marlon Brando in The Wild One, denim became a symbol of teenage rebellion.

Schools across the U.S. banned students from wearing jeans, claiming they promoted delinquency. Some movie theaters turned away customers who showed up in denim.

The bans only made jeans more popular. By the 1960s, they were embraced by rock stars, activists, and youth movements.

Radioactive socks. Snail-based dye. A perfume born from a measurement error. Jeans that got you banned from school. Fashion has always been stranger than it looks.

CHAPTER FOURTEEN

MODERN MUSICIANS

TAYLOR SWIFT LITERALLY SAVED A RECORD STORE FROM CLOSING

Most celebrities sell albums. Taylor Swift saved an entire store.

In 2020, the pandemic nearly shut down Grimey's, a beloved independent record store in Nashville. With sales plummeting, the shop was on the verge of closing for good.

Then Taylor Swift quietly stepped in and paid the salaries of every employee. No press, no grand announcement. Just a behind-the-scenes act of kindness that kept the store alive.

Grimey's co-owner later said it was completely out of the blue. She just wanted to help. The store survived and is still open today.

Taylor has long been known for giving back, whether it's secretly paying off student loans, surprising fans with concert tickets, or donating millions to education and disaster relief.

The store didn't know the sweet gesture was coming. That seems to be how she prefers it.

THE TIME BEYONCÉ REHEARSED IN HEELS FOR 11 HOURS STRAIGHT

Beyoncé isn't just called Queen Bey for her vocals. Her work ethic is on another level.

During rehearsals for a major performance, Beyoncé spent 11 straight hours practicing in high heels. While most people would have collapsed after a few hours, she kept going, making sure every move, every note, and every detail was right.

For her Coachella performance, she spent eight months training like an athlete, sticking to a strict diet and rehearsing nonstop to deliver a show so iconic that fans renamed the festival "Beychella."

THE BEATLES WROTE AND RECORDED AN ENTIRE ALBUM IN LESS THAN 24 HOURS

In 1963, before The Beatles became the biggest band in the world, they were four young musicians racing against the clock. Their debut album, Please Please Me, was recorded in a single day: 13 tracks, 10 of which were laid down in one marathon session. With a limited budget and tight studio time, the band played for nearly 13 hours straight.

By the end of the session, John Lennon had nearly lost his voice. He powered through one last take of "Twist and Shout" anyway. His strained, raspy vocals became one of the most iconic moments in rock history. Producer George Martin later said that Lennon's voice was so shredded that another take would have been impossible.

That recording still exists. You can hear his voice giving out in real time.

Dolly Parton Uses "I Will Always Love You" Royalties in a Loving Way

Dolly Parton didn't just write one of the most iconic love songs of all time. She also used it to change lives.

In 1973, Dolly wrote "I Will Always Love You" as a farewell song to her longtime mentor and business partner. When Elvis Presley wanted to record it, his manager insisted that Presley receive half the song's publishing rights.

Dolly refused. It was one of the hardest decisions of her career, but it paid off two decades later when Whitney Houston's version became a global phenomenon, earning Dolly millions in royalties.

Instead of spending the money on herself, she quietly invested it into a Black business district in Nashville, helping to revitalize the community where Houston grew up.

She never mentioned it publicly. Someone else did.

PRINCE PLAYED 27 INSTRUMENTS ON HIS FIRST ALBUM

Most musicians start their careers with a band. Prince was the band.

At 19 years old, Prince recorded his debut album, For You, in 1978, playing every single instrument on it. All 27, including guitar, bass, piano, drums, synthesizers, and orchestral strings. He didn't just contribute to the music. He created every note, layering each instrument himself.

He also produced the entire album, a rare feat for any artist, let alone a teenager making his industry debut. He spent long hours in the studio ensuring every sound met his standards.

Nobody else was in the room. He didn't need them to be.

MICHAEL JACKSON'S BEST-SELLING ALBUM IS STILL STRONG

Michael Jackson didn't just release an album. He created a global phenomenon.

Thriller, released in 1982, became the best-selling album in history, with over 70 million copies sold worldwide. Decades later, it's still selling. It was the first album certified triple diamond by the RIAA, 30x platinum in the U.S. alone.

Game-changing music videos, genre-blending sounds, and a dance that's still performed today. "Billie Jean," "Beat It," and "Thriller" didn't just top the charts. They changed the entire music industry.

Dolly turned down Elvis. Prince played 27 instruments at 19. Michael Jackson's album is still selling 40 years later. The bar is somewhere in the stratosphere.

CHAPTER FIFTEEN

THE MIND-BENDING WORLD OF SCIENCE

Volcanic Lightning: Nature's Fiery Light Show

When a volcano erupts, you expect lava, ash, and plumes of smoke. Sometimes the sky also cracks open with lightning.

Volcanic lightning, also known as a "dirty thunderstorm," is a rare phenomenon where bolts of lightning emerge from thick volcanic ash clouds. It happens when volcanic particles collide, generating static electricity and triggering powerful electrical discharges.

One of the most famous occurrences happened during the eruption of Mount Sakurajima in Japan, where bright white flashes lit up the dark ash cloud. Another was the 2010 eruption of Iceland's

Eyjafjallajökull, which disrupted air travel across Europe. Scientists captured images of lightning arcing through the ash plume.

Unlike lightning in thunderstorms, which forms due to differences in temperature and moisture, volcanic lightning arises from the chaotic interactions of charged ash particles, ice crystals, and volcanic gases. Scientists are still studying it, hoping to better understand eruptions and potentially predict them.

PRINCE RUPERT'S DROPS: GLASS THAT DEFIES LOGIC

Take a piece of glass that can withstand a hammer blow, but shatters completely if you snap its tail. That's a Prince Rupert's Drop.

These teardrop-shaped pieces of glass are made by dripping molten glass into cold water. The rapid cooling creates immense internal tension, compressing the outer layer while leaving the inside under extreme stress. That combination makes the bulbous end strong enough to resist bullets.

The tail is another story. Snap it, and the entire structure explodes into dust in a fraction of a second, releasing all that stored energy at once.

Scientists studied Prince Rupert's Drops for centuries without fully understanding them. It took modern high-speed cameras and stress analysis technology to work out the physics. Research on these drops has since influenced the development of tempered glass and military armor.

SUPERFLUIDITY: THE LIQUID THAT DEFIES GRAVITY

What if a liquid could climb walls, leak through solid containers, and flow endlessly without losing energy? That's superfluidity, one of the strangest quantum phenomena ever observed.

Superfluidity occurs when helium is cooled to just a few degrees above absolute zero (-273.15°C or -459.67°F). At this extreme temperature, helium stops behaving like a normal liquid. It enters a quantum state where its atoms move in perfect harmony, without friction or resistance. It can crawl up and over the sides of containers. It can flow in an endless loop without slowing down. It can escape through microscopic pores in solid surfaces as though the container isn't there.

Scientists first discovered superfluidity in the 1930s, but its bizarre properties continue to be studied. Some theories suggest that neutron stars, the collapsed cores of massive stars, behave like gigantic cosmic superfluids. Research into superfluidity is influencing quantum computing, nanotechnology, and theories about the fundamental nature of space and time.

THE MANY-WORLDS INTERPRETATION: ARE THERE INFINITE PARALLEL UNIVERSES?

What if every decision you make creates a new reality? According to the Many-Worlds Interpretation of quantum mechanics, this might not be science fiction. It could be the nature of reality itself.

The theory suggests that every time a quantum event occurs, the universe splits into multiple parallel worlds, each representing a different possible outcome. Tiny particles don't behave predictably. They exist in superposition, meaning they can be in multiple states at once. When observed, they appear to choose a single outcome. In the Many-Worlds Interpretation, all possible outcomes happen, just in different universes. Flip a coin: one universe exists where it lands on heads, another where it lands on tails. Apply that to every particle interaction in existence, and the number of alternate realities becomes infinite.

While impossible to test directly, the theory has real implications for physics and philosophy. It also means that somewhere, in another reality, a version of you made different choices and is living a completely different life.

Quantum Entanglement: The Universe's Strangest Connection

Two particles, linked so completely that a change in one instantly affects the other, no matter how far apart they are. Even across the galaxy. That's quantum entanglement.

Entanglement happens when two quantum particles interact in such a way that they become paired. Once entangled, their states remain connected regardless of distance. If one changes, the other changes instantly. Albert Einstein called it "spooky action at a distance." He wasn't a fan. Decades of experiments have since confirmed it's real.

The implications are significant. In theory, entanglement could allow for instantaneous communication across vast distances, with applications in computing and cryptography. Scientists are exploring how it might enable quantum teleportation, transferring information without it physically traveling through space. Quantum entanglement is already shaping the future of secure communications and quantum computing.

WHITE HOLES: THEORETICAL TIME-REVERSED BLACK HOLES

Black holes devour everything in their path. But what if they had a mirror opposite, an object that couldn't be entered and only pushed matter and light outward? That's a white hole.

A white hole is a black hole in reverse. Instead of pulling everything inward, it would constantly eject matter and energy, making it impossible for anything to enter. No white hole has ever been observed, but the idea comes from Einstein's general theory of relativity, which suggests that if black holes can exist, their mathematical opposites could too.

Some physicists believe the Big Bang itself may have been a massive white hole, an event where all the matter in the universe erupted into existence at once. Others speculate that white holes could connect to black holes through wormholes, potential shortcuts through space-time.

Nobody has ever seen one. The math says they should exist, and that's currently all we have.

Helium climbs walls. Glass explodes from its own tail. Two particles share a state across the galaxy. The universe is not behaving itself.

CHAPTER SIXTEEN

STRANGE MOMENTS
IN MUSIC HISTORY

THE DAY A SYMPHONY ORCHESTRA WAS
CONDUCTED BY A CAT

I n 2007, a cat named Nora became a viral sensation after videos showed her sitting at a piano and pressing the keys. Lithuanian composer Mindaugas Piečaitis was so fascinated by her musical instincts that he composed a piece for her, called CATcerto. Instead of a human soloist, the performance featured Nora playing via video while a live orchestra performed alongside her.

A legitimate orchestral concert where the featured pianist was a cat.

THE SILENT SYMPHONY THAT BECAME A HIT

In 1952, composer John Cage premiered one of the most controversial pieces in music history: 4'33", a composition where musicians sit in total silence for four minutes and 33 seconds.

No instruments, no melodies. Just silence. The audience, confused at first, realized the "music" was the ambient sound of the concert hall itself. The coughs, the shuffling, the room.

4'33" became one of the most famous avant-garde pieces ever written. It has since been performed with full orchestras, solo pianos, and rock bands.

It has been performed thousands of times. Nobody has ever played a wrong note.

THE TIME A FAN'S ASHES WERE SENT TO A KISS CONCERT

Some fans buy merch. Others get tattoos. One KISS superfan arranged to have his ashes blasted into the air at a concert.

KISS is known for over-the-top stage shows, but in 2021, frontman Gene Simmons revealed that a fan's family had sent his cremated remains in a container labeled "KISS Forever." The request was to have the ashes incorporated into the band's pyrotechnic effects.

Whether the band followed through is unclear. Simmons and Paul Stanley have confirmed it wasn't the first time they'd received such a request. The band also launched a $5,000 "KISS Kasket" package for fans who want to spend eternity in a KISS-themed coffin.

THE BAND THAT SENT IMPOSTORS TO THEIR OWN PRESS CONFERENCE

In 1969, American rock band The Turtles were supposed to attend a press conference. They had a better idea. Instead of showing up, they sent actors dressed like them to take their place.

The fake band answered reporters' questions, posed for photos, and signed autographs, all while the real Turtles watched from the audience.

Nobody noticed. The impostors made it through the entire event without being exposed.

THE POP SONG THAT WAS SO CATCHY, IT GOT BANNED

In 2013, South Korean girl group Crayon Pop released their ultra-catchy hit "Bar Bar Bar." The song had an infectious beat, repetitive lyrics, and a dance that went viral.

The South Korean government banned it from radio.

Officials claimed the repetitive beat and high-energy rhythm could cause traffic accidents by making drivers too distracted or excited.

The ban only made it more popular.

THE ROLLING STONES HIRED THE HELLS ANGELS AS SECURITY — BAD IDEA

In 1969, The Rolling Stones planned a free concert at Altamont Speedway in California, aiming to recreate the peaceful atmosphere of Woodstock. It did not go that way.

They hired the Hells Angels motorcycle gang as security and paid them in beer.

As the crowd grew restless, the Angels clashed violently with fans, hitting them with pool cues and motorcycle chains. During The Rolling Stones' set, a man in the audience pulled a gun. The Hells Angels stabbed him to death.

The entire event was captured in the documentary Gimme Shelter. Many historians consider it the end of the hippie era.

A cat performed with an orchestra. A band watched their own fake press conference from the back of the room. A free concert ended in a stabbing. Music history has range.

CHAPTER SEVENTEEN

SPORTS DEFEATS

SERENA WILLIAMS WON THE AUSTRALIAN OPEN WHILE PREGNANT

Winning a Grand Slam is one of the toughest achievements in sports. Doing it while eight weeks pregnant is something else entirely.

In 2017, Serena Williams entered the Australian Open without telling anyone she was pregnant. Despite her body already undergoing major changes, she didn't drop a single set throughout the entire tournament. She reached the final against her sister Venus and won her 23rd Grand Slam title, breaking the Open Era record for most major singles titles.

Only after the tournament did the world find out she had done it while carrying her first child.

Talk about a winner.

THE "RUMBLE IN THE JUNGLE": MUHAMMAD ALI SHOCKED THE WORLD (1974)

Going into the 1974 heavyweight title fight, George Foreman was considered unstoppable. He had never lost a professional fight, had knocked out both Joe Frazier and Ken Norton in two rounds each, and hit hard enough that his punches were compared to getting hit by a truck.

Muhammad Ali was seen as past his prime. A 32-year-old underdog facing a younger, stronger, heavily favored champion.

Ali had a plan.

Instead of trading punches with Foreman, he invented the "rope-a-dope": leaning against the ropes, letting Foreman swing wildly, absorbing blows while conserving energy. By round eight, Foreman was exhausted. Ali struck back and knocked him down for the first time in his career, winning by knockout.

THE LEICESTER CITY MIRACLE: THE 5,000-TO-1 CHAMPIONS (2016)

Before the 2015-16 Premier League season, nobody took Leicester City seriously. The year before, they had barely escaped relegation. Their odds of winning the league were 5,000 to 1, the same odds as Elvis being found alive.

Under coach Claudio Ranieri, they stunned the world anyway. Their players, most considered average or unwanted by bigger clubs, defeated Manchester United, Chelsea, and Liverpool. Jamie Vardy's record-breaking goal streak and goalkeeper Kasper Schmeichel's saves pushed them deeper into title contention than anyone thought possible.

When they secured the championship, even rival fans had to acknowledge it.

THE 2007 SUPER BOWL: THE GIANTS STUN THE UNDEFEATED PATRIOTS

FLAG: Minor fact check. The 2007 season ended in Super Bowl XLII, played in February 2008. The chapter title calls it "the 2007 Super Bowl" but that would be Super Bowl XLI. Worth clarifying which you mean so it's accurate for readers.

The 2007 New England Patriots were supposed to be unstoppable. They had won every game that season, 16-0, had the greatest offensive duo in the NFL in Tom Brady and Randy Moss, and were expected to crush the New York Giants in Super Bowl XLII.

The Giants barely made the playoffs. Nobody gave them a chance.

The Giants shut down the Patriots' record-breaking offense and held them to just 14 points. The defining moment came with under two minutes left. Giants quarterback Eli Manning escaped three defenders, launched a deep pass, and receiver David Tyree caught it by pinning the ball against his helmet while falling to the ground. That catch set up the game-winning touchdown. Final score: Giants 17, Patriots 14.

The perfect season was over.

THE BOSTON RED SOX'S HISTORIC COMEBACK: OVERCOMING A 3-0 DEFICIT

In baseball history, no team had ever come back from a 3-0 deficit in a playoff series.

In 2004, the Boston Red Sox did it against their biggest rival, the New York Yankees.

After losing the first three games of the American League Championship Series, the Red Sox were on the brink of elimination. In Game 4, down 4-3 in the ninth inning, they pulled off a stolen base that changed the momentum, tied the game, and eventually won in extra innings. In Game 5, another extra-inning victory.

By Game 6, ace pitcher Curt Schilling took the mound with a torn ankle tendon, his sock soaked in blood. The Red Sox won again, forcing a winner-takes-all Game 7. Boston dominated, winning 10-3 and completing the first-ever 3-0 series comeback in Major League Baseball history.

They didn't stop there. The Red Sox swept the St. Louis Cardinals in the World Series, ending an 86-year championship drought.

SIMONE BILES MAKES OLYMPIC HISTORY AGAIN AND AGAIN

Simone Biles has won more World Championship medals than any gymnast in history.

In 2021, she attempted a move no other female gymnast had ever tried in competition: the Yurchenko double pike vault. Done incorrectly, it could cause serious injury. She landed it.

After taking time off for mental health and recovery, she returned in 2023 and won her eighth all-around U.S. gymnastics title, the most in history.

The Patriots were 16-0. The Red Sox were three games from elimination. Leicester City was one season from the second division. None of it mattered in the end. The scoreboard doesn't care about the odds.

CHAPTER EIGHTEEN

NO PLACE LIKE HOME

THE DISHWASHER WAS INVENTED BY SOMEONE WHO NEVER DID DISHES

Most people invent things to solve their own problems. The modern dishwasher is an exception.

In 1886, Josephine Cochrane, a wealthy socialite, was frustrated that her servants kept chipping her expensive china. She invented a machine that would wash it for them.

Her design used water pressure instead of scrubbing, making it more efficient than handwashing. Initially dishwashers were only used in hotels and restaurants. After World War II they became common household appliances.

Cochrane became the first woman to receive a U.S. patent for a kitchen appliance. She probably never loaded one herself.

TOILETS FLUSH DIFFERENTLY DEPENDING ON THE HEMISPHERE — OR DO THEY?

It's one of the most popular myths out there: toilets flush in different directions in the Northern and Southern Hemispheres because of the Coriolis effect.

The Coriolis effect is real. It affects weather patterns, ocean currents, and hurricanes, making them rotate counterclockwise in the Northern Hemisphere and clockwise in the Southern Hemisphere.

It doesn't affect toilets.

The swirling direction of toilet water is determined by the design of the toilet and the angle of the jets, not the Earth's rotation. The Coriolis effect is powerful enough to influence massive weather systems. It is not powerful enough to control a few gallons of water in a bowl.

VACUUM CLEANERS USED TO BE SO BIG THEY NEEDED HORSES

Today, vacuum cleaners are compact, sleek, and even robotic. In the early 1900s, they had to be pulled by horses.

The first motorized vacuum, invented in 1901 by Hubert Cecil Booth, was called the "Puffing Billy" and was the size of a wagon. Homeowners didn't buy them. They hired vacuum services, where an operator would park the machine outside, run hoses through windows, and suck dust from inside the house.

These early vacuums were so expensive that only the very wealthy could afford them. Some services turned cleaning into a public event, with crowds gathering to watch the giant hoses pull dust off furniture.

It took decades before vacuum cleaners became portable and small enough to fit in a closet.

THE FIRST ALARM CLOCK COULD ONLY RING AT 4 AM

The first mechanical alarm clock could only wake you up at one specific time.

Invented in 1787 by an American named Levi Hutchins, it could only be set to ring at 4 AM. Why? Because that's when Hutchins needed to wake up for work. He didn't bother making it adjustable.

It wasn't until 1847 that a French inventor created a mechanical alarm clock that let people set their own wake-up times.

WHY DOORKNOBS USED TO BE MADE OF BRASS

Brass doorknobs weren't just a style choice. Brass has natural antibacterial properties. Germs touching a brass surface don't survive long. Studies have found brass can kill bacteria within hours, while plastic and steel can let germs survive for days.

Before modern cleaning products, this was an unintentional but effective way to slow disease spread. Some hospitals and public buildings still use brass fixtures for exactly this reason.

REFRIGERATORS WERE ONCE FILLED WITH TOXIC GASES

Your refrigerator keeps food safe today. In the early 1900s, it could have killed you.

Early fridges were cooled with dangerous gases like ammonia, methyl chloride, and sulfur dioxide. Leaks were common. The results were sometimes deadly.

By the 1920s, enough fatal accidents had occurred that scientists developed a safer refrigerant called Freon. Freon turned out to be terrible for the environment, which led to the eco-friendly refrigerants used today.

Levi Hutchins only needed 4 AM. Josephine Cochrane only needed her china intact. Hubert Cecil Booth needed a horse. The modern home got built one specific problem at a time.

CHAPTER NINETEEN

DON'T UNDERESTIMATE YOUR DOGS AND CATS

A BLOODHOUND'S SENSE OF SMELL CAN BE USED AS LEGAL EVIDENCE IN COURT

With over 300 million scent receptors, compared to a human's 5 million, Bloodhounds have one of the most powerful noses in the animal kingdom. They can track a scent over 130 miles and follow trails that are more than two weeks old.

Their accuracy is so reliable that in many jurisdictions, a Bloodhound's scent-tracking results are admissible as evidence in court. Their work has helped solve crimes, locate missing persons, and exonerate the wrongly accused.

CATS HAVE A BUILT-IN GPS THAT SCIENCE CAN'T FULLY EXPLAIN

Cats don't just find their way home. They can navigate hundreds of miles through places they have never been.

There are documented cases of cats traveling across entire states to reunite with their owners. One cat, Holly, went missing in Florida and turned up 200 miles away, two months later, back at home.

Scientists still don't fully understand how they do it. Some theories suggest cats use the Earth's magnetic field, similar to migratory birds. Others believe their sense of smell allows them to track familiar scents across long distances.

Nobody has a definitive answer.

DOGS CAN HEAR SOUNDS FOUR TIMES FARTHER THAN HUMANS

Dogs can hear sounds from four times farther away than humans and detect frequencies up to 65,000 Hz, compared to the human limit of around 20,000 Hz. They pick up high-pitched noises we can't perceive at all: dog whistles, the ultrasonic calls of small rodents, even early seismic activity before earthquakes hit.

Some breeds, like Border Collies and German Shepherds, can learn to recognize over 200 words.

CATS CAN MAKE OVER 100 DIFFERENT SOUNDS

Forget "meow." Cats have a much wider range than that.

While dogs communicate primarily through barks, whines, and growls, cats can produce over 100 distinct sounds: meows, purrs, chirps, trills, and more. They also develop unique meows tailored specifically for human interaction, adjusting pitch and tone to communicate with their owners.

That chattering sound cats make when they spot a bird through the window is something else entirely. Some experts think it mimics prey sounds or signals excitement. Others think it's frustration. Either way, your cat is doing something specific, and it's probably not random.

DOGS HAVE BEEN TRAINED TO DETECT DISEASES LIKE CANCER AND DIABETES

Dogs can detect deadly diseases with their noses.

Medical detection dogs are trained to identify certain illnesses, including cancer, diabetes, malaria, and Parkinson's disease. Studies show they can detect cancer cells in a person's breath, urine, or sweat with up to 97% accuracy, sometimes before medical tests can.

For people with diabetes, alert dogs are trained to recognize changes in their owner's scent when blood sugar levels drop too low or spike too high. They nudge, paw, or fetch emergency supplies before a dangerous episode occurs.

Some hospitals and research labs now use trained dogs to screen patients.

A Cat's Purr Can Help Heal Bones and Reduce Stress

A cat's purr is not just soothing. It may actually be therapeutic.

When cats purr, they produce vibrations at frequencies between 25 and 150 Hz. Studies have shown that sound frequencies in this range can promote healing in bones and tissues, potentially aiding in the repair of fractures, reduction of swelling, and healing of infections. It may explain why cats seem to recover quickly from injuries and why they purr when hurt or stressed.

For humans, the sound of a purr can reduce stress and lower blood pressure. Some studies suggest it can help decrease symptoms of difficulty breathing in both cats and their owners.

Dogs are screening for cancer. Cats are navigating by magnetic field. Bloodhounds are testifying in court. They seemed like pets. Turns out that was the underestimate.

CONCLUSION

Before you know it, we're here at the end, full of cool new facts.

You've learned about a tennis match that broke the scoreboard, secret rooms hidden in famous landmarks, and even a man who ate an entire airplane. Those are just a few of my favorites. I'm sure you've found your own.

So, what now?

Now, you share.

Start a conversation. Drop a fact.

The world's too strange, too surprising, and too endlessly fascinating to ever stop collecting facts. New things are discovered every day. Weird coincidences unfold. Unexpected friendships form.

Like a full fridge on a hot day, the more cool stuff you've got stocked in your brain, the easier it is to keep things chill.

Now go surprise someone.

THANK YOU FOR READING

ALSO AVAILABLE ON AUDIBLE

If you enjoyed Yo, Sloth. I Got the Facts,

a quick review on Amazon means

more than you know.

Just a few words about what made you

smile, laugh, or say, "Wait... what?"

It helps the next curious reader find their way here.

You can search the title on Amazon, or simply scan the code below:

Thank you.

Truly.

Eddie

COMPLETE SERIES
BY EDDIE WATTS

SERIOUSLY THOUGH BOOKS

All three available on Amazon

ALSO AVAILABLE ON AUDIBLE

Straight from the Llama's Mouth:

The Curious Origins and Clever Meanings of Idioms and Phrases

Arrested for What Now:

A Global Guide to Bizarre Laws, Bans, and Moves You Never Knew Were Illegal

SOURCES

Andrews, E. (2016, August 19). The heist that made the Mona Lisa famous. History. https://www.history.com/news/the-heist-that-made-the-mona-lisa-famous

Angus, S. D. (2018). A statistical timetable for the sub-2-hour marathon: Insights from a diffusion model. Medicine & Science in Sports & Exercise, 50(8), 1787–1793. https://doi.org/10.1249/MSS.0000000000001616

Auto Europe. (n.d.). Driving on the Autobahn in Germany: Must-read tips & info. https://www.autoeurope.com/travel-guides/germany/driving-the-autobahn-in-germany/

Baum, L. F. (1900). *The Wonderful Wizard of Oz*. George M. Hill Company.

BBC News. (2013). London skyscraper 'Walkie-Talkie' blamed for melting car. https://www.bbc.com/news/uk-england-london-23930675

BBC News. (2001). Pizza Hut delivers to space for $1 million. https://www.bbc.com

Behnke, S. A., Thomas, R. J., McNutt, S. R., Krehbiel, P. R., & Rison, W. (2013). Observations of volcanic lightning during the 2009 eruption of Redoubt Volcano. *Journal of Volcanology and Geothermal Research, 259*, 214-234. https://doi.org/10.1016/j.jvolgeores.2012.04.011

Bekenstein, J. D. (2003). Information in the holographic universe. Scientific American, 289(2), 58-65.

Bell, J. S. (1964). On the Einstein-Podolsky-Rosen paradox. *Physics Physique Физика, 1*(3), 195-200. https://doi.org/10.1103/PhysicsPhysiqueFizika.1.195

Bennett, A. T. D., Cuthill, I. C., & Partridge, J. C. (1996). Ultraviolet vision and mate choice in birds. Nature, 380(6573), 433-435.

Biles, S. (2021). *Courage to Soar: A Body in Motion, a Life in Balance*. Zondervan.

Bradshaw, J. W. S. (2013). *Cat sense: How the new feline science can make you a better friend to your pet*. Basic Books.

Bright, R. (2018). *Beneath the Magic: The hidden Tunnels of Disney World*. Theme Park Press.

Burns, R. (1785). To a mouse. John Wilson.

Cage, J. (1952). *4'33" and the Concept of Silence in Music*. Wesleyan University Press.

Carroll, S. (2016). *The Big Picture: On the Origins of Life, Meaning, and the Universe Itself*. Dutton.

Chang, R. (2020, March 2). *Dr. Seuss wrote 'Green Eggs and Ham' on a bet*. Biography.

https://www.biography.com/authors-writers/dr-seuss-green-eggs-and-ham-bet

Chaucer, G. (1971). *Troilus and Criseyde* (N. Coghill, Trans.). Penguin Classics. (Original work published c. 1380)

Chaucer, G. (2005). *The Canterbury Tales* (J. Mann, Ed.). Penguin Classics. (Original work published c. 1390)

Chelenza, L. (2015, October 7). Have a chatty cat? They are capable of expressing over 100 sounds. Spectrum News. https://spectrumlocalnews.com/tx/austin/pet-pointers/2015/10/7/chatty-cats-

Cicero. (1999). *Letters to Atticus* (D. R. Shackleton Bailey, Trans.). Harvard University Press. (Original work published 1st century BC)

Cohen, C. (2004). *Dr. Seuss and his Literary Challenges: The Story Behind Green Eggs and Ham*. Random House.

Comune di Venezia. (n.d.). *Forbidden behaviour*. Retrieved from https://www.comune.venezia.it/en/content/comportamenti-vietati

Coren, S. (2000, March 1). Sleep deprivation, psychosis and mental efficiency. Psychiatric Times. https://www.psychiatrictimes.com/view/sleep-deprivation-psychosis-and-mental-efficiency

Cox, L. (2004). *Swimming to Antarctica: Tales of a Long-Distance Swimmer*. Knopf.

Crystal, D. (2004). *The Stories of English: Shakespeare's Linguistic Legacy*. Oxford University Press.

Cytowic, R. E. (2018). *Synesthesia: A Union of the Senses* (2nd ed.). MIT Press.

Damasio, A. R. (1995). Neurological disorders and visual perception: A study on spatial dyslexia. Journal of Neuropsychology, 12(3), 221-234.

Damasio, H., & Damasio, A. (1989). Phineas Gage: The man who changed neuroscience. Journal of Neuropsychology, 27(4), 203-219.

Davies, H. (2001). *The Beatles: The Definitive Story of Their Music and Legacy*. HarperCollins.

DeWitt, B. S. (1970). Quantum mechanics and reality. *Physics Today, 23*(9), 30-35. https://doi.org/10.1063/1.3022331

Donnelly, R. J. (2009). The two-fluid theory and second sound in liquid helium. *Physics Today, 62*(10), 34-39. https://doi.org/10.1063/1.3225507

Dorsey, L. (2019). **Hidden history of World War II in Seattle**. University of Washington Press.

Dowson, E. (1894). Non sum qualis eram bonae sub regno cynarae. The Bodley Head.

Duncan, D. E. (1998). *Calendar: Humanity's Epic Struggle to Determine a True and Accurate Year*. Avon Books.

Ebbesmeyer, C., & Scigliano, E. (2009). *Flotsametrics and the Floating World: How One*

Man's Obsession with Runaway Sneakers and Rubber Ducks Revolutionized Ocean Science. HarperCollins.

EF Tours Blog. (2008, May 15). *Venice bans pigeon feeding*. Retrieved from https://blog.eftours.com/article/venice-pigeon-feeding-ban/

Einstein, A., Podolsky, B., & Rosen, N. (1935). Can quantum-mechanical description of physical reality be considered complete? *Physical Review, 47*(10), 777-780. https://doi.org/10.1103/PhysRev.47.777

Eichar, D. (2013). *Dead mountain: The Untold True Story of the Dyatlov Pass Incident*. Chronicle Books.

Endler, J. A., & Mielke, P. W. (2005). *Comparing Color Patterns as Birds See Them*. Biological Journal of the Linnean Society, 86(4), 405-431.

ESPN. (2009, March 3). Minor leaguer traded for bats meets tragic end. https://www.espn.com/mlb/news/story?id=3950464

Everett, H. (1957). "Relative State" formulation of quantum mechanics. *Reviews of Modern Physics, 29*(3), 454-462. https://doi.org/10.1103/RevModPhys.29.454

Fadiman, C. (2006). *The World Treasury of Modern Quotations*. Hachette Books.

Feinstein, J. S., Adolphs, R., & Tranel, D. (2010). The human amygdala and the biology of fear: Case study of patient SM. Nature Neuroscience, 13(6), 807-813.

Fitzherbert, J. (1534). *The Boke of Husbandry*. Thomas Berthelet.

Franklin, B. (1733-1758). *Poor Richard's Almanack*. Self-published.

Frolov, V. P., & Novikov, I. D. (1998). Black hole physics: Basic concepts and new developments. Springer Science & Business Media.

Garcia, M. (2020, February 6). Christina Koch completes 328-day mission in space. NASA. https://www.nasa.gov

Gibson, D. E. (2001). The man who ate everything: A study on pica and human adaptation. Journal of Unusual Physiology, 32(2), 147-159.

Gleick, J. (2011). *Genius: The Life and Science of Richard Feynman*. Pantheon Books.

Graham, J. B., & Lee, H. J. (2004). *Air-Breathing Fishes: Evolution, Diversity, and Adaptation*. Academic Press.

Gray, D. (2019). *The Wow! Signal: Searching for Alien Messages in the Cosmos*. HarperCollins.

Greene, B. (2011). *The Hidden Reality: Parallel Universes and the Deep Laws of the Cosmos*. Knopf.

Guinness World Records. (2021, May 12). 56-year-old freediver holds breath for almost 25 minutes breaking record. https://guinnessworldrecords.com/news/2021/5/freediver-holds-breath-for-almost-25-minutes-breaking-record-660285

Hahn, L. (2017). Prince: A life in music. Backbeat Books.

Hanlon, R. T., & Messenger, J. B. (2018). *Cephalopod Behavior and Camouflage Mechanisms*. Cambridge University Press.

Harriss, J. (2015). The Eiffel Tower's secret apartment: Gustave Eiffel's hidden hideaway. Journal of Architectural History, 27(3), 112-124.

Hauser, T. (2000). *Muhammad Ali: His life and times.* Simon & Schuster.

Hawking, S. W., & Ellis, G. F. R. (1973). The large scale structure of space-time. Cambridge University Press.

Heller, J. (1961). *Catch-22.* Simon & Schuster.

Hesiod. (1988). *Works and Days* (M. L. West, Trans.). Oxford University Press. (Original work published 8th century BC)

Hill, J. M., Hogan, J. D., & Smith, M. J. (2016). Stress distribution in Prince Rupert's drops: A high-speed polariscope study. *Journal of Applied Physics, 119*(15), 154903. https://doi.org/10.1063/1.4946123

Hogwood, C. (2013). *Handel and Bach: The Greatest Meeting That Never Happened.* Oxford University Press.

Hohn, D. (2011). *Moby-Duck: The True Story of 28,800 Bath Toys Lost at Sea.* Viking.

Homer. (1990). *The Iliad* (R. Fagles, Trans.). Penguin Classics. (Original work published 8th century BC)

Howard, K. (2010). *Rock & Roll's Greatest Pranks: The Stories Behind Music's Wildest Moments.* HarperCollins.

Hubbard, E. M., & Ramachandran, V. S. (2005). Neurocognitive mechanisms of synesthesia. Neuron, 48(3), 509-520.

Hugo, V. (1862). *Les Misérables.* Pagnerre Press.

Ishimatsu, A., & Graham, J. B. (2011). Mudskippers: Amphibious fishes and their adaptations to land. Marine Biology Review, 78(2), 215-235.

Jamieson, A. J., & Yancey, P. H. (2019). Life at the deepest point on Earth: New discoveries in the Mariana Trench. Marine Biology Journal, 18(2), 321-340.

Jet Propulsion Laboratory. (2011, August 3). LEGO figurines aboard Juno. NASA. https://www.jpl.nasa.gov/images/pia14413-lego-figurines-aboard-juno

Jönsson, K. I., Rabbow, E., Schill, R. O., Harms-Ringdahl, M., & Rettberg, P. (2008). *Tardigrades survive exposure to space in low Earth orbit.* Current Biology, 18(17), R729–R731. https://doi.org/10.1016/j.cub.2008.06.048

Kandel, E. R. (2013). *Principles of Neural Science* (5th ed.). McGraw-Hill.

Kapitza, P. L. (1938). **Viscosity of liquid helium below the λ-point**. *Nature, 141*(3558), 74-75. https://doi.org/10.1038/141074a0

Keep Talking Greece. (2017, October 31). Why you can't wear high heels at ancient sites in Greece. https://www.keeptalkinggreece.com/2017/10/31/greece-ancient-sites-high-heels/

Kellogg, C. (2008, February 27). *Did Hemingway really write his famous six-word story?* Los Angeles Times. https://www.latimes.com

Kerscher, J., & Sachs, G. (2016). The science of stomach acid: Functions and protective mechanisms. Journal of Physiology & Biochemistry, 72(4), 657-672.

King, M. (2017). *The Leicester Miracle: How a 5,000-to-1 Underdog Won the Premier League*. HarperCollins.

Kindy, D. (2019, January 23). The accidental invention of bubble wrap. Smithsonian Magazine. https://www.smithsonianmag.com/innovation/acciden tal-invention-bubble-wrap-180971325/

Kobayashi, M., Kikuchi, D., & Okamura, H. (2009). Imaging of ultraweak spontaneous photon emission from human body displaying diurnal rhythm. PLOS One, 4(7), e6256.

Legends and myths regarding the Titanic. (2023, September 15). *Wikipedia*. Retrieved from https://en.wikipedia.org/wiki/Legends_and_myths_regard ing_the_Titanic

LePort, A., Stark, C. E., & McGaugh, J. L. (2012). Highly superior autobiographical memory: Case study of Jill Price and the neuroscience of memory. Neuroscience Journal, 18(4), 301-312.

Lewisohn, M. (2013). **The Beatles: All these years, volume one – Tune in**. Crown Archetype.

Lovell, M. (2009). *Amelia Earhart: The Sound of Wings*. St. Martin's Griffin.

Lubow, A. (1992, November 22). *Hemingway didn't say that*. The New York Times. https://www.nytimes.com

MacDonald, I. (2005). **Revolution in the head: The Beatles' records and the sixties**. Chicago Review Press.

Maldacena, J. (1999). The large N Limit of Superconformal Field Theories and Supergravity. International Journal of Theoretical Physics, 38(4), 1113-1133.

Martell, L. J., & Collins, A. G. (2021). The Evolutionary Mystery of the Immortal Jellyfish. Current Biology, 31(5), R171-R173.

Massachusetts Humane Society. (2022, May 30). Ask a vet with Dr. Sam: Is it true that cats only meow at humans? https://mrfrs.org/ask-a-vet-with-dr-sam-cats-only-meow-at-humans/

Mather, J. A., & Kuba, M. (2013). The intelligent octopus: Problem-solving and camouflage. Marine Biology, 160(6), 1847-1860.

Mazzeo, T. J. (2010). *The Secret of Chanel No. 5: The Intimate History of the World's Most Famous Perfume*. HarperCollins.

McCrum, R., MacNeil, R., & Cran, W. (2010). *The story of English*. Penguin Books.

McNally, A. (2012). Survival in extreme cold: The science behind Lynne Cox's open-water feats. Journal of Cold-Weather Physiology, 24(3), 237-251.

Melville, H. (1851). *Moby-Dick*. Harper & Brothers.

Méndez Harper, J., & Dufek, J. (2016). **The electrification of volcanic plumes**. *Science Advances, 2*(4), e1501800. https://doi.org/10.1126/sciadv.1501800

Metcalf, P., & Huntington, R. (1991). *Celebrations of Death: The Anthropology of Mortuary Ritual*. Cambridge University Press.

Milton, J. (1634). *Comus.* Humphrey Moseley.

Mitchell, M. (1936). *Gone with the wind.* Macmillan.

Mokhtar, M. (2022). **Glass drops and their extreme properties**. *Materials Today, 54*(3), 112-119. https://doi.org/10.1016/j.mattod.2022.04.008

Montgomery, S. (2014). *The Secret Life of the Sloth: Lessons in Slow Survival.* Simon & Schuster.

Moore, R. (2013). **The Walkie-Talkie skyscraper: A melting pot of architectural missteps**. *The Guardian*. https://www.theguardian.com/artanddesign/2013/sep/06/london-walkie-talkie-skyscraper-melting-cars

Mow, V. C., & Huiskes, R. (2005). *Basic Orthopaedic Biomechanics and Mechano-Biology.* Lippincott Williams & Wilkins.

Musicians of the Titanic. (2023, September 15). *Wikipedia.* Retrieved from https://en.wikipedia.org/wiki/Musicians_of_the_Titanic

NASA Jet Propulsion Laboratory. (n.d.). *The Golden Record.* NASA. https://voyager.jpl.nasa.gov/golden-record/

National Aeronautics and Space Administration. (2023). We are made of stardust: How the universe created you. https://www.nasa.gov

National Archives. (2022). **World War II camouflage efforts: The fake Boeing town**. U.S. National Archives and Records Administration. https://www.archives.gov/military/world-war-ii/camouflage-seattle

National Geographic. (2023). Do parallel universes exist? The physics behind the Many-Worlds Interpretation. https://www.nationalgeographic.com/science/article/many-worlds-interpretation

National Geographic. (2023). How unbreakable glass drops shatter at a single touch. https://www.nationalgeographic.com/science/article/prince-rupert-drops

National Geographic. (2022). Meet the jellyfish that can cheat death. https://www.nationalgeographic.com

National Geographic. (2023). Quantum entanglement: How "spooky action at a distance" is reshaping physics. https://www.nationalgeographic.com/science/article/quantum-entanglement

National Geographic. (2023). The quantum mystery of superfluidity explained. https://www.nationalgeographic.com/science/article/superfluidity-quantum-physics

National Geographic. (2023). What is volcanic lightning and how does it form? https://www.nationalgeographic.com/environment/article/volcanic-lightning-explained

National Geographic. (2023). What are white holes? The hypothetical cosmic opposites of black holes. https://www.nationalgeographic.com/science/article/white-holes-physics

National Geographic. (2023). **What's really hidden behind Mount Rushmore?** https://www.nationalgeographic.com/travel/article/mount-rushmore-hall-of-records

National Hurricane Center Archives. (n.d.). Compiled data on tropical storms and hurricanes. National Oceanic and Atmospheric Administration.

National Institute of Diabetes and Digestive and Kidney Diseases. (2022). How the digestive system works. https://www.niddk.nih.gov

National Museum of American History. (2023). Microwave ovens: A kitchen revolution. https://americanhistory.si.edu

National Oceanic and Atmospheric Administration. (2022). Tracking ocean currents using plastic debris. https://www.noaa.gov

National Park Service. (2022). The Hall of Records: Mount Rushmore's hidden chamber. U.S. Department of the Interior. https://www.nps.gov/moru/learn/historyculture/hall-of-records.htm

National Public Radio. (2013). How The Beatles made 'Please Please Me' in a single day. https://www.npr.org/sections/therecord/2013/02/11/171717133/how-the-beatles-made-please-please-me-in-a-single-day

Norman, M. D. (2000). *Cephalopods: A World Guide.* ConchBooks.

North, T. (1579). *Plutarch's Lives.* Richard Field.

NPR. (2009, May 18). Heels, food banned from ancient Greek sites. https://www.npr.org/2009/05/18/104239042/heels-food-banned-from-ancient-greek-sites

Nyad, D. (2015). *Find a way: The inspiring story of one woman's perseverance.* Knopf.

Online Etymology Dictionary. (n.d.). (D. Harper, Ed.). https://www.etymonline.com

Orwell, G. (1949). *1984.* Secker & Warburg.

Osorio, D., & Vorobyev, M. (2008). A review of color vision in birds. Journal of Experimental Biology, 211(11), 1803-1810.

Overbury, T. (1613). *A Wife.* Thomas Creede.

Parton, D. (2017). *Dolly on Dolly: Interviews and Encounters.* Chicago Review Press.

Pauli, J. N., Peery, M. Z., & Ribeiro, M. C. (2014). Algae symbiosis in sloths: Camouflage and nutritional benefits. Proceedings of the Royal Society B, 281(1780), 20133000.

Pendergrast, M. (2010). *Uncommon Grounds: The History of Coffee and How it Transformed Our World.* Basic Books.

Perrault, C. (1697). *Cendrillon, Ou La Petite Pantoufle De Verre.* Claude Barbin.

Piccard, J., & Walsh, D. (1962). *Seven Miles Down: The Story of the Bathyscaphe Trieste.* Putnam.

Piraino, S., De Vito, D., & Schmid, V. (1996). Reversing development in immortal jellyfish. Nature, 381(6581), 315-319.

Pliny the Elder. (1938). *Natural history* (H. Rackham, Trans.). Harvard University Press.

(Original work published 77 AD)

Purrfect Post. (n.d.). Healing purrs: How your cat can help you heal. https://www.purrfectpost.com/healing-purrs-how-your-cat-can-help-you-heal/

Quarles, F. (1635). *Emblemes.* John Marriott.

Rattanawong, S. (2019). Monkeys and tourism in Thailand: Cultural significance and human-wildlife interactions. Southeast Asian Journal of Cultural Studies, 14(2), 89-105.

Raytheon Technologies. (2021). The accidental invention of the microwave. https://www.rtx.com

Reuters. (2008, April 30). *Venice to fine tourists who feed pigeons.* Retrieved from https://www.reuters.com/article/lifestyle/venice-to-fine-tourists-who-feed-pigeons-idUSL30700279/

Richardson, J. (2019). *The science of taste: How food tasters shape the pet industry.* HarperCollins.

Rolling Stone. (2022). How Prince recorded his debut album and played every instrument. https://www.rollingstone.com/music/music-news/prince-for-you-album-making-of-1218742/

Rothen, N., Meier, B., & Ward, J. (2012). Enhanced Memory Ability in Synesthetes: The role of contextual and pictorial elaboration. Neuroscience & Biobehavioral Reviews, 36(8), 1952-1959.

Rousseau, J. J. (1765). *Confessions.* Marc-Michel Rey.

Schatzkin, P. (2002). *The man who shocked the world: The life and times of Percy Spencer.* Walker & Company.

Scott, W. (1816). *The antiquary.* Archibald Constable.

Sealed Air Corporation. (2023). The history of bubble wrap. https://www.sealedair.com

Sender, R., Fuchs, S., & Milo, R. (2016). Revised estimates for the number of human and bacterial cells in the body. PLOS Biology, 14(8), e1002533.

Shakespeare, W. (1984). *Romeo and Juliet* (G. B. Evans, Ed.). Cambridge University Press. (Original work published 1595)

Shakespeare, W. (1997). *Othello* (E. A. J. Honigmann, Ed.). Arden Shakespeare. (Original work published 1604)

Shakespeare, W. (1998). *Julius Caesar* (D. Daniell, Ed.). Arden Shakespeare. (Original work published 1599)

Shakespeare, W. (2002). *King Henry IV, Part 1* (D. S. Kastan, Ed.). Arden Shakespeare. (Original work published 1597)

Shakespeare, W. (2005). *The tempest* (F. Kermode, Ed.). Cambridge University Press. (Original work published 1611)

Shakespeare, W. (2008). *Hamlet* (G. R. Hibbard, Ed.). Oxford University Press. (Original work published 1603)

Shen, V., & Turner, C. H. (2006). Bone strength and mechanics: Why bones are stronger than they seem. Journal of Bone and Mineral Research, 21(6), 949-957.

Simmons, G. (2021). *Rock & roll forever: The wildest stories behind KISS.* HarperCollins.

Sing, D. K., et al. (2016). Detection of high-speed winds on HD 189733b using transmission spectroscopy. Nature, 529(7584), 59-62.

Smith, C. (2021). The mermaid economy: Inside the world of professional mermaids. Journal of Performing Arts, 38(2), 87-103.

Smith, L. (2007). *Not Quite What I Was Planning: Six-Word Memoirs by Writers Famous and Obscure.* Harper Perennial.

Smithsonian Magazine. (2017). How a melted chocolate bar led to the invention of the microwave. https://www.smithsonianmag.com

Smithsonian Magazine. (2023). How a London skyscraper accidentally melted cars with sunlight. https://www.smithsonianmag.com/innovation/skyscraper-melt ing-cars-london-180987234/

Smithsonian Magazine. (2023). How Seattle built an entire fake city to protect Boeing's wartime aircraft production. https://www.smithsonianmag.com/his tory/seattles-hidden-wwii-camouflage-123456789

Smithsonian Magazine. (2021). The secret room behind Mount Rushmore that few people know about. https://www.smithsonianmag.com/history/mount-rush more-hidden-hall-of-records-180968864/

Société d'Exploitation de la Tour Eiffel. (n.d.). Did Gustave Eiffel live in the Tower? https://www.toureiffel.paris/en/news/130-years-did-gustave-eiffel-live-tower

Standage, T. (2006). *A History of the World in 6 Glasses.* Walker & Company.

Steele, V. (2017). *Shoes: A History from Sandals to Sneakers.* Oxford University Press.

Steele, V. (2019). *The corset: A Cultural History of Restrictive Fashion.* Oxford University Press.

Steinbeck, J. (1937). *Of mice and men.* Covici-Friede.

Stephenson, B. (2020). *The history of timekeeping and calendars.* Cambridge University Press.

Stevenson, R. L. (1886). *Strange case of Dr. Jekyll and Mr. Hyde.* Longmans, Green & Co.

Stromberg, J. (2013, October 2). This alkaline African lake turns animals into stone. Smithsonian Magazine. https://www.smithsonianmag.com/science-nature/ this-alkaline-african-lake-turns-animals-into-stone-445359/

Susskind, L. (2005). *The Cosmic Landscape: String Theory and the Illusion of Intelligent Design.* Little, Brown.

Swift, J. (1738). *A Complete Collection of Polite and Ingenious Conversation.* Charles

Bathurst.

TA Landscape Architecture. "Golden Bridge Ba Na Hills." TA Landscape Architecture, talavn.com.vn/golden-bridge-bana-hills.

Taraborrelli, J. R. (2009). *Michael Jackson: The Magic, the Madness, the Whole Story.* Grand Central Publishing.

Taub, R. (2004). Liver regeneration: From myth to mechanism. Nature Reviews Molecular Cell Biology, 5(10), 836-847.

The Bible. King James Version. (1611). https://www.biblegateway.com

Tobias, A. (2010). *Beneath the Neon: Life and Death in the Tunnels of Las Vegas.* Huntington Press.

Tripp, N. (2017, December 27). The haunting effects of going days without sleep. NPR. https://www.npr.org/2017/12/27/573739653/the-haunting-effects-of-going-days-without-sleep

Tudahl, D. (2018). Prince and the Purple Rain Era Studio Sessions: 1983 and 1984. Rowman & Littlefield.

Turner, D. C., & Bateson, P. (2013). *The domestic cat: The biology of its behavior.* Cambridge University Press.

U.S. Soccer. (2019, June 11). USA surges to World Cup record 13-0 win in opening match against Thailand. https://www.ussoccer.com/stories/2019/06/usa-surges-to-world-cup-record-13-0-win-in-opening-match-against-thailand

Vatican Archives. (1582). Gregorian calendar reform documents. https://www.vatican.va

Virginia Beach Veterinary Hospital. (2023, July 13). The therapeutic benefits of a cat's purr. https://vbvh.net/blog/the-therapeutic-benefits-of-a-cats-purr/

Wallace Hartley. (2023, September 15). *Wikipedia.* Retrieved from https://en.wikipedia.org/wiki/Wallace_Hartley

Warhol, A. (1968). Art and mass media commentary. Random House.

Wikipedia contributors. "Golden Bridge (Vietnam)." Wikipedia, The Free Encyclopedia, en.wikipedia.org/wiki/Golden_Bridge_(Vietnam).

Wilde, O. (1890). *The Picture of Dorian Gray.* Ward, Lock & Co.

Willis, C. (2016). *The Empire State Building: Secrets of New York's Tallest Icon.* HarperCollins.

Withals, J. (1616). *A Short Dictionary for Young Beginners.* Richard Tottell.

Wolff, C. (2000). *Johann Sebastian Bach: The Learned Musician.* W.W. Norton & Company.

Zamoyski, A. (2010). *Chopin: Prince of the Romantics.* HarperCollins.

Zoological Studies on Bees & Pollination. (1980-Present). Research from the Smithsonian Institution & University of Cambridge.

www.ingramcontent.com/pod-product-compliance
Lightning Source LLC
Chambersburg PA
CBHW070343130626
46556CB00007B/3009